JOSH McDOWELL

The Secret of Loving

*How a lasting
intimate relationship
can be yours*

Here's Life Publishers

P.O. Box 1576, San Bernardino, CA 92402-1576

THE SECRET OF LOVING
by Josh McDowell

Published by
HERE'S LIFE PUBLISHERS, INC.
P. O. Box 1576
San Bernardino, CA 92402

ISBN 0-89840-099-6
HLP Product No. 951103

Unless indicated, Scripture quotations are from the New American Standard Bible, © The Lockman Foundation 1960, 1962, 1963, 1968, 1971, 1972, 1973, 1975, and are used by permission. Other Scripture quotations are from The Living Bible (TLB), the Phillips translation, and the Amplified Version of the New Testament.

Library of Congress Cataloging in Publication Data

McDowell, Josh.
    The secret of loving.

    Bibliography: p.
    1. Love (Theology)   I. Title.
BV4639.M37 1985   248.4   85-7655
ISBN 0-89840-099-6

FOR MORE INFORMATION, WRITE:

L.I.F.E. — P.O. Box A399, Sydney South 2000, Australia
Campus Crusade for Christ of Canada — Box 300, Vancouver, B.C., V6C 2X3, Canada
Campus Crusade for Christ — 103 Friar Street, Reading RGI IEP, Berkshire, England
Lay Institute for Evangelism — P.O. Box 8786, Auckland 3, New Zealand
Great Commission Movement of Nigeria — P.O. Box 500, Jos, Plateau State Nigeria, West Africa
Life Ministry — P.O. Box/Bus 91015, Auckland Park 2006, Republic of South Africa
Campus Crusade for Christ International — Arrowhead Springs, San Bernardino, CA 92414, U.S.A.

CONTENTS

DEDICATION

To Jim and Doris Youd, my father- and mother-in-law, with deep affection, respect, and appreciation for modeling to their children the secret of loving. Gratefully, my family and I will benefit for the rest of our lives because of their love and example.

FOREWORD

Frequently I am asked, "Isn't it hard on your marriage, having Josh travel so much?" Or someone suggests, "Doesn't your relationship suffer because of Josh's busy speaking schedule?"

I'll admit I'd love to have Josh home more—but having him home every evening would not change the quality of our marriage. Josh demonstrates over and over, in lots of creative ways, that the children and I are his top priority, whether he is with us or not. Knowing and experiencing that gives us a deep sense of security that we wouldn't trade for anything! You see, Josh lives out on a daily basis what he shares in this book about love, marriage, sex and parenting.

Granted, an excellent marriage relationship takes effort. From the beginning, Josh has given 150 percent to making our marriage the most exciting I can image. Not surprisingly, I have loved giving him 150 percent in return.

In this book Josh shares from his heart and his research what he has learned about being the right person as a husband or wife. He also provides eleven keys to a mature love relationship. I know they will work for you because they are working for us.

Dottie McDowell

SECTION I

YOU ARE THE SECRET!

How to Be the Right Person in a Loving Relationship

SOMETHING MORE

Working late one night my concentration was broken by the insistent ring of the telephone.

"Mr. McDowell?"

An obviously depressed young woman hardly waited for me to respond.

"Mr. McDowell, during the last five nights I have been to bed with five different men. Tonight I just sat alone on the bed after it was over and said to myself, 'Is that all there is to it?'" Her voice breaking with tears, she concluded, "Please tell me there is something more."

"There is," I replied. "It's called intimacy."

Maybe like that young woman you are asking yourself right now, "Is that all there is?" You thought you were getting a relationship and discovered your date was looking for a night out. You are married and you long for a candlelight dinner, and the best you can get out of your mate is a few grunts as he watches the football game. Maybe you are already separated or divorced and as you look back you ask, "Is that all there is?"

If that is the question you are asking, you are not alone. The search for true love is the theme of most hit songs and runs as an undercurrent through almost every movie. It is the lifeblood of thousands of pop novels consumed by millions of people. Megadollars fuel advertising campaigns built solely on our desire for intimacy. The soaps and sitcoms both reflect and rekindle our dreams. And if you really want to be a winner as a speaker, put on a seminar about techniques for succeeding at love, sex and marriage.

When I visit university campuses I am guaranteed a crowd when the promotion proclaims as the topic "Maximum Sex." Though I use a less provocative theme when I speak to church young people, I know any talk on love and sex gets the crowds.

The fact you are reading this book proves that our massive preoccupation with finding real love is largely unsuccessful. True love remains elusive at best. The bestselling columnist and author, Dr. Leo Buscaglia, writes, "We've gone full circle. We've gone into leaving the family, leaving the moral values, leaving all things that are good, the things we call platitudes. We've tried everything—sexual promiscuity, multi-marriages. But we find that all those things have just left us feeling alone and empty. So now we're beginning to look again at those old-fashioned values and to recognize that perhaps there is some truth in them."[1]

Sex Isn't Enough

You and I know that one of those old-fashioned values is intimacy. Ann Landers had an incredible response when she asked, "Would you prefer snuggles instead of sex?" More than 64,000 out of 90,000 who responded affirmed, "A warm hug or gentle touch is more important than intercourse."[2] Though I am not convinced that those who responded truly preferred one over the other, those who responded clearly expressed a craving for intimacy in a sexual relationship.

Had a hug today? Then you will agree with Dr. Jerome Sherman when he said, "Being human, we do want the warmth; the closeness. It's a basic human desire. Sex in and of itself is mechanical."[3]

Yet is that really true of men as well? Aren't men supposed to be mainly interested in sexual activity?

"The results are accurate," acknowledges Dr. Joyce Brothers, nationally-recognized psychologist, speaking of the results of Ann Landers' question. "For a long, long time—back to the Victorian era—men and women have had sex in order to get the touching or cuddling. We have a touch hunger and sex is the coin that people pay for affection."[4]

We really know very little about love and sex, don't we? The national divorce rate is but one indicator that we have a long way to go before we unlock the mysteries. Even the specialists in the field acknowledge that.

"Research has hardly even begun to dabble in the problems of love and love affairs," confesses Dr. John Money of Johns Hopkins University, a recognized sex and gender specialist. "It's just much easier to talk about sex. But what human beings are really concerned with is love and the human relationship."[5]

Bankrupt Freedom

In my counseling with hundred of couples I have found that the biggest problem is not Victorian repression. Instead, couples confess that the joy and passion have gone out of sex. This finding is backed up by sex therapists like Rollo May, who writes in *Love and Will*: "...

therapists today rarely see patients who exhibit repression of sex.... In fact, we find in the people who come for help just the opposite: a great deal of talk about sex, a great deal of sexual activity, practically no one complaining of cultural prohibitions over going to bed as often or with as many partners as one wishes. But what our patients do complain of is lack of feeling and passion. 'The curious thing about this ferment of discussion is how little anyone seems to be enjoying emancipation.' So much sex and so little meaning or even fun in it!"[6]

Technique Is Not the Answer

Nor is more detailed information on the mechanics of sex and birth control the answer. World-renowned sex therapists William Masters and Virginia Johnson acknowledge that "of all the recent notions about sex that have been given publicity in recent years, none is more harmful than the idea that a poor sexual relationship can be 'cured' by learning technique from a book—any book.... An emphasis on the importance of technique is characteristic of so much that passes for good advice today. Nothing good is going to happen in bed between a husband and wife unless good things have been happening between them before they get into bed. There is no way for good sexual technique to remedy a poor emotional relationship. For a man and a woman to be delighted with each other in bed, both must want to be in bed— with each other."[7]

The real need today is for the capacity to put back into relationships the passion, joy and intimacy that will last. Instead, most people are willing to give time, energy and money to becoming a better sex partner but neglect the nurture of the essential skills of caring, loving and sharing. When new techniques fail, responsibility and commitment, if given equal amounts of time and energy, will restore the intimacy and joy so essential in marriage.

Getting the Order Right

You can describe marriage as a "love, marriage and sex relationship." This is simply putting in order the process by which a fulfilling relationship develops between a man and a woman. Throughout this book we will highlight the values and qualities essential to a lasting relationship and marriage so you can begin to focus on them instead of sexual prowess. This will help you avoid the many tempting but deadend "shortcuts" to love and intimacy. And it will help you join your partner in embracing the essential values and qualities that will help you avoid the trap of sexual promiscuity— or divorce, if married.

This book could be described as a two step process. First we will explore your individual qualities, what you need to be so you are the right kind of person in a loving relationship. You see, the secret of loving is *being the right person* for someone else. In the second part of this book we will examine the attributes of genuine love—the only lasting force in a relationship. The secret of maximum love, marriage and sex is a mature love expressed in a committed relationship.

The Tyranny of Fear

Two fears, I believe, keep many people from experiencing the intimacy and joy of this lasting relationship.

One is the fear of never being loved.

The other is the fear of never being able to love.

The primary reason these fears exist is a breakdown of love as it is being modeled in our homes. We do not develop habits of genuine love automatically. We learn them by watching effective role models— most specifically by observing how our parents express love for each other day in and day out.

The fact is, "love is as vital as calories" in the growing up years, says Dr. Benjamin Spock. In his keynote address to the Mid-Century White House Conference on Children and Youth, he insisted, "This is not just sentimental talk. It is a fact that infants who have long been starved for company and affection...may wither in body and spirit. They lose all joy in doing things and seeing people....Such tragedies are rare, but they prove that love is as vital as calories."

After spending a great deal of time working with emotionally disturbed young people, Dr. Leo Buscaglia wrote that there are "people who have literally given up at that young age because they really have not experienced love. They don't know how to share it, they don't know how to give it, they don't know how to receive it. If you reach out to them, they scream, go through tantrums—'Don't touch me.'" He concludes," It's a hard path, and some of them never come back."[8]

Such people often grow up emotionally handicapped, lacking any capacity to receive love or to give it. They cannot give what they do not have. On the other hand, the more love we have received freely from our parents, the more we can allow ourselves to share love. But we have to be on the receiving end of it first.

It is also important that a child believes not only that "my parents love me," but that "my parents love each other." For when children miss seeing love modeled in the home, they grow up without really knowing how to give or receive love.

Today many of us have grown up without this instructive, parental model. As a result we consciously or unconsciously fear entering into a relationship as close as marriage. If this love model was missing in your home, if you have never learned how to love, the thought of having to love someone else and live with that person for the rest of your life becomes awesome and scary. Even though you crave the warmth and intimacy of a deep, loving relationship, you frequently find yourself backing off. You may even turn tail and run from an emotional involvement that appears to be pointing toward marriage.

One student expressed his fear of love this way: "Before I became a Christian, I was afraid that I would never be loved. What was more frightening was that I did not know if I would ever be able to love anyone...I knew I used people. In all my relationships I had some ulterior motives. As a result, I could never get close to anyone."

A 16-year-old who saw my TV special, "The Secret of Loving," expressed her fear this way: "I had decided that I would never know true love. I felt that I would never be able to cope with a relationship."

There Is Hope

The program gave her new hope: "I saw your program, and it showed me that it wasn't impossible for me to have someone really love me." This is the hope we have built into this book—you can overcome the fear and become a mature lover despite your inadequate preparation for love.

Even Leo Buscaglia sounds a note of hope: "Most of us have another chance. In fact, every day presents the possibility of another chance."[9]

Yet this book will not only afford you a second chance—it will help you make the best of your first chance. If you are a high school young person or a single adult, you will find a gameplan that will help you become the person you want to be—one capable of giving and receiving mature love. Even if you bought the idea that sex is the "super glue" that binds a lasting relationship, and you got burned in the process, there is hope for you.

The material in this book will help you objectively answer the questions: "Am I personally ready for marriage?" and "Is our love mature enough to sustain a fulfilling, lifelong marriage and sexual relationship?" Now if you haven't begun asking these questions, you need to.

If you are already married, the research and insights presented here will help you understand how various areas of your life and your relationships can be developed and improved upon so you can build toward a satisfying and truly intimate marriage.

Finally, if you are a parent, counselor, pastor, teacher, or one who works with young people or singles, these truths will help you share the personal qualities and attitudes necessary for enjoying a lasting and intimate love, marriage and sex commitment.

Ready for the adventure of your life? You can begin right now to become the right person for a life of mature love.

Questions to Ponder

- What are you looking for in a relationship?
- What will give you a lasting marriage relationship?
- What fear is preventing you from achieving intimacy?

LOOKING FOR MR. RIGHT

What qualities do you consider most important in the man of your dreams? What kind of person do you think will make a good lover?

A recent survey by *Family Journal* magazine revealed that sensitivity tops the list for many women today. The macho man is actually considered a poor risk by most of those who responded to the survey.

Some of us get downright particular about the person who supposedly will make us happy. At a singles conference in Portland, Oregon, a woman clearly in her late 20's approached me and said, "Mr. McDowell, let me show you the type of man I want to marry." With a flourish she unfolded a list of forty-nine traits she was looking for in a man.

"Lady," I said after scanning her list, "You don't want a husband, you want Jesus."

Yet not only is it women who develop lists of what they are looking for. At the University of Washington a sophomore approached me, whipped out his diary, and said, "Let me show you the type of woman I want to marry." Of the fourteen qualities on his list I recall only faithfulness and trustworthiness.

This time I took a different approach.

"Let me ask you a question," I said. "How do *you* score on those fourteen points?"

"What do you mean?" he asked.

"The qualities you are looking for in a wife," I said. "Are they found in your own life?"

I could see I had him thinking.

"It's not so much finding the right person," I continued, "but being the right person that counts in marriage. If you want a queen, you need to be a king. If you want a good lover, you need to be a good lover."

Discovering the secret of loving is much like looking for your glasses, only to find them perched on your head, or looking for your key ring and discovering it in your hand. Most of us search and search for the right person, when all the while the key is being the right person. So many are out looking when they ought to be working...on becoming the right kind of person.

Yet how can we become the right person? First, it is important that we recognize that our love life will always be a reflection of our character qualities.

You Become the Standard

When someone comments, "There aren't any good men or women around," I always reply, "The problem may be with you, not with the shortage of good men or women." I recognize this may be rather strong medicine for some, but the fact is that good men and women gravitate to other good men and women.

Reinforcing this, sociologists Dr. Evelyn Duvall and Dr. Reuben Hill write, "When you come to marriage, what do you bring? A new wardrobe? A nest egg in the bank? Some furniture you've inherited? A dependent relative or two? A good job and the prospect of advancement? Whatever your tangible assets or liabilities are, there is something even more important: that is you as a personality, the way you act toward people and the attitudes you bring to marriage.

"The kind of marriage you make depends upon the kind of person you are. If you are a happy, well-adjusted person, the chances are your marriage will be a happy one . If you have made adjustments so far with more satisfaction than distress, you are likely to make your marriage and family adjustments satisfactorily. If you are discontented and bitter about your lot in life, you will have to change before you can expect to live happily ever after."[1]

Duvall and Hill conclude that much of the unhappiness in marriages has been blamed on choosing the wrong marriage partner, money problems, sexual adjustments, or religion. In reality, they say, unhappiness stems from what you have brought into the marriage.[2]

They emphasize the need to come to marriage "prepared to mean a great deal to your chosen one. Success in your marriage relationship is dependent on bringing to the union the habit of happiness and the capacity to love and be loved. These attributes of an emotionally mature personality are the best possible dowry you can bring to a marriage."

This is underscored in *Your Life Together* by Elof Nelson: "Success in marriage is more than finding the right person. Being the right person is even more important. I have found that young people I counsel with are looking for the perfect mate without being much concerned about the person their mate is getting."[3]

If you desire to marry a terrific person, then you must be a terrific person yourself. And the process of discerning just what personal areas you might need to improve upon is simple. Make a list of the qualities you want in a mate. Then, one by one, measure yourself against that list.

Marriage can only be a give and take commitment; you must be willing to give exactly what you want to receive. As one therapist shared, "There are two things that cause unhappy marriages—men and women!"

Deserving What We Get

We get what we deserve. Though overdone for emphasis, author Bob Phillips' description[4] of the contrast between what we look for and what we get is not really so far off.

The Ideal Wife
What Every Man Expects

- Always beautiful and cheerful. Could have married movie stars, but wanted only you. Hair that never needs curlers or beauty shops.
- Beauty that won't run in a rainstorm. Never sick—just allergic to jewelry and fur coats.
- Insists that moving furniture by herself is good for her figure.
- Expert in cooking, cleaning house, fixing the car or TV, painting the house, and keeping quiet.
- Favorite hobbies: mowing the lawn and shoveling snow.
- Hates charge cards.
- Her favorite expression: "What can I do for you, dear?"
- Thinks you have Einstein's brain but look like Mr. America.
- Wishes you would go out with the boys so she could get some sewing done.
- Loves you because you're so sexy.

What He Gets

- She speaks 140 words a minute with gusts up to 180.
- She once was a model for a totem pole.
- A light eater—as soon as it gets light, she starts eating.
- Where there's smoke, there she is—cooking.
- She lets you know you only have two faults: everything you say and everything you do.
- No matter what she does with it, her hair looks like an explosion in a steel wool factory.
- If you get lost, open your wallet—she'll find you.

The Ideal Husband
What Every Woman Expects

- He will be a brilliant conversationalist.

- A very sensitive man—kind and understanding, truly loving.
- A very hard-working man.
- A man who helps around the house by washing dishes, vacuuming floors, and taking care of the yard.
- Someone who helps his wife raise the children.
- A man of emotional and physical strength.
- A man who is smart as Einstein, but looks like Robert Redford.

What She Gets

- He always takes her to the best restaurants. Some day he may even take her inside.
- He doesn't have any ulcers; he gives them.
- Anytime he has an idea in his head, he has the whole thing in a nutshell.
- He's well-known as a miracle worker—it's a miracle when he works.
- He supports his wife in the manner to which she was accustomed— he's letting her keep her job.
- He's such a bore that he even bores you to death when he gives you a compliment.
- He has occasional flashes of silence that makes his conversation brilliant.

Of course you get the point. The golden rule of a successful marriage might be stated something like: Whatever qualities you desire in a mate, develop first in yourself.

Building a caring, loving and fulfilled marriage relationship takes time and work. In fact, development will continue for a lifetime. It simply takes real effort for the selfish behavior patterns acquired during dating to be transformed into the kind of selfless love that underlies a good marriage.

As you read the following chapter keep in mind two questions: 1) What type of person should I be? 2) What qualities should I build into my life to work toward a fulfilled love, marriage and sexual relationship? A good self-image is certainly the starting point. Let's look at how healthy yours is.

Questions To Ponder

- Why do you think it is important to be proud of the one you love?

CHAPTER 3

A PROPER SELF-PORTRAIT

Have you ever shown someone the photos in your purse or wallet? Around the dining room tables in my graduate school, for example, girlfriends were a frequent topic of conversation. I happened to be dating a very attractive young lady, so I proudly whipped open my billfold to show off Connie's picture. All the guys would ooh and aah...and so did I.

Frequently parents, and certainly grandparents, cannot wait for friends to ask about pictures of the children or grandchildren. With blinding speed and unbridled enthusiasm the photos go on display.

Well...most of them do. Usually there is one picture they do not want to show anyone. And you protect yours with equal zeal. Before there's half a chance of it surfacing, you whisk your driver's license photo out of sight. It is the ugliest, most embarrassing photo of you in captivity. And you're probably convinced, as I am, that the state goes out of its way to catch us with the sourest, most unflattering looks possible on our faces.

Traumatic as that may be, every one of us carries about another portrait of ourselves with far greater importance than the image on our driver's license. It's what psychologists call our self-image—the mental picture we have of ourselves. This image alone daily determines how you and I perceive ourselves before other people.

Wouldn't it be interesting if our faces and bodies were to be somehow altered so that others would see us in the same way we actually view our real selves? The mere thought would send most of us into a cold sweat. Yet in a way that really happens, for by the time we reach middle age our faces (and often our bodies) are a surprising reflection of what we think of ourselves.

Who Do You Think You Are?

To set the stage for our discussion of self-image I want to ask you two questions.

1. How much are you worth? I don't mean in terms of dollars and cents, but what you are worth as a person.
2. Are you glad for and excited about who you are? Do you really feel good about yourself?

The conscious or unconscious ways you daily answer these questions determine your choices, your values, your responses and attitudes—basically the way you live your life. The opinions we hold of ourselves affect everything we do.

Dr. Robert C. Kolodney of the Masters and Johnson Institute in St. Louis, for example, reports that less than ten percent of a couple's therapy is focused on the physical part of the relationship, even though this is why the couple thought they came for help. Ninety percent of the therapy is focused on the areas of self-esteem and interpersonal communication.[1]

Your self-image affects not only the way you see yourself, but how you relate to your parents, your friends, your spouse, and God. The Old Testament writer of Proverbs provides the clue in chapter 23 verse 7, when he writes, "As a man thinketh, so he is." Thus it is not what you say or how you appear on the outside that determines what you do. It is the way you think of yourself deep down inside—the way you feel at "gut level"—that motivates your actions.

Psychologists usually refer to a person as having a "high or low, good or bad" self-image. I prefer to call it a "healthy" or "unhealthy" self-image. Whatever the label, the real questions are: What is a healthy self-image? How should we perceive ourselves?

If you have read the New Testament letters of the apostle Paul, you will agree that he does not take a back seat to anyone. Yet he also wrote that the believer is to "not think more highly of himself than he ought to think" (Romans 12:3). Now Christians frequently take this to mean they should not think highly of themselves. But that was not Paul's meaning at all. He said we are not to think "*more highly*" than we ought to think.

Well then, how are we to think? Paul clears this up in the same verse. We are to "Think so as to have sound judgment." Put simply, this is seeing ourselves from God's perspective—no more, no less. "No more" so we are not led into pride, and "no less" so we do not fall into false humility. So if you are going to think according to sound judgment, you will need to perceive yourself from the biblical perspective.

Stop for a moment to analyze how you feel and think about yourself. Would you, for example, much rather be someone else? If so, your perspective may need changing. With all my serious limitations, I cannot honestly think of anyone else on the face of this earth I would rather be than me. Which says something about the way God has helped me see the assets, strengths and abilities He has placed in me.

Spiritual Vertigo

To help us all get a proper self-portrait we need to put into practice several biblical principles. For some of you this may be a new idea, but *the truest thing about you is what God says about you in His word, the Bible.* Your emotions, your culture, or your feelings cannot dictate who you are. If you allow them to, you can be misled easily. Sometimes I feel so close to God that I am certain I could not get any closer. At other times I am tempted to believe my negative feelings when they tell me that a great distance exists between God and me. I am faced with deciding whether to believe my feelings or accept what the Bible says about the reality of God.

When Jesus said, "Lo, I am with you always" (Matthew 28:20), or "I will never desert you, nor will I ever forsake you" (Hebrews 13:5), I prefer to believe Him instead of my feelings.

It's much like a strange phenomenon called vertigo sometimes experienced in flying. When a small plane passes through dense fog or clouds, or is caught in a severe storm blotting out visual references to the horizon, a pilot can drop a wing tip severely without realizing it. He may *feel* certain that he is flying level. But the only way he can know for sure is to watch his instruments, which do not lie.

The pilot's five senses—everything he can see, hear, feel, touch and taste—may be telling him that everything is perfectly fine. However, if he is an experienced pilot, he knows he can be profoundly fooled and will force himself to trust his instruments. They are his only reliable guide to ultimate reality. Pilots who fail to exercise this discipline seldom live to get a second chance.

Every day in my Christian life I experience a kind of "spiritual vertigo." Maybe I'm running short on sleep or exercise; maybe someone offended me and it has affected my emotions. They are leading me to one conclusion and course of action. But the word of God shows me another, and it is at that moment that I have a crisis of choice: Which guide to reality am I going to believe?

As with the pilot, indecision can be lethal. It can put me on a spiritual "rally"coaster—rallying, then coasting; rallying, then coasting. One moment I'm up, and the next I'm down. But when I come to my senses and commit myself to the principle that the truest thing about me is what God says about me, I get off the rallycoaster and begin growing again toward maturity in my experience of Christ.

Remember the last time you worked on a jigsaw puzzle? The best way to proceed is to use the picture on the box top as your guide. I remember a close friend of mine, Dick Day, telling me about a fellow who bought two puzzles as birthday gifts for a relative who dearly loved puzzles. Before he wrapped them he switched the box tops. Can you imagine the frustration?

Yet that's how many Christians today are trying to put the puzzle of their lives together—with the wrong box top as their guide. The box top of emotions is sitting where the box top of God's Word, the Bible, should be. The predictable result is sheer, fruitless frustration.

So let's check our instruments. Let's look again at our spiritual box top. Let's review some of the things God says are true about you.

What Are You Really Worth?

Have you ever said, "I really don't count. I could disappear and no one would notice or care"? Most people think those thoughts at one time or another. Yet the Bible reveals that God looks at us quite differently. In the Bible, God tells you that He sees you as very special because *God created you in His image.*

Right at the start of the Old Testament, Genesis 1, we read that God said, "Let us make man in our image." So He did it. This accounts for our ability to love, to exercise our will, to choose and make moral decisions. Most of us have not really stopped to think about how special that is.

Suppose you went outside and stood next to a tree. You could say that in many ways you are equal in value to the tree, since both you and the tree were specially created by God. But there is one critical difference—God created you in His image. God did not give His image to any other part of His creation.

You are special also because *you are of great value and worth to God.* In 1 Corinthians 6, Paul says that we have been purchased with a great price. The value or worth of an object is usually determined by the price one is willing to pay to purchase or redeem it. It couldn't be more true for you or me. When someone asks what I am worth, I can factually say that that I am worth the price God paid for me, which was "Jesus."

Before I became a Christian, this realization really humbled me. If I had been the only person alive, Jesus Christ still would have died for me. He would have died for you if you had been the only one who needed it. A young lady in Dallas, Texas, said, "Josh, I believe that's true. But that means that I would have been the only one there to drive the spikes through His hands to crucify Him."

Without question you are special and of great value. In Matthew 6:26 Jesus emphasizes this. His followers were having a problem. They were concerned with what they should wear, what they were going to eat and drink, and where they were going to sleep. And Jesus selected the birds to illustrate His point. He explained that birds don't reap; they don't gather into barns. He said, "Your heavenly Father feeds them." Have you ever seen a sparrow starve? Then Jesus drove the obvious point home: "Are you not worth much more than they?"

I am amazed at how many people seem to think they are not worth even the value of a sparrow. God has made you of great value. And the real basis for a healthy self-image is to understand and accept the value God has placed on you.

As you ponder this truth, be careful to recognize that it is not because of any merit on your part. Your value and worth is based not upon what you have done, but upon who Jesus is and what He has done for you. Christ's loving actions on your behalf have demonstrated and documented forever the great value you have to God.

Better Than One In a Million?

Another reason you are special is because *you are unique*. Of the four and a half billion people alive right now on this planet, there is no one just like you. If out of four and a half billion people there is only one you, why in the world would you want to be like someone else? Yet most people go through life envious of others—their things, their physique, their hair, or their talents and abilities. You must begin fixing your thoughts on the fact God has made you unique and that, as one person put it, "God don't make no junk."

After one of my lectures on uniqueness a young man wrote a poem titled simply, "Me." It made this profound point: If I spend all my time being someone else; who is going to spend their time being me? Now think about that. If you spend all your time being someone else, who is going to spend their time being you? God created only you to be you and no one can be you better. From eternity past to eternity future there never has been and never will be another person like you. And once you realize how incredibly unique this makes you, you can stop the deadly practice of comparing yourself to other people.

People sometimes ask me why I don't do things like Chuck Swindoll. Or why I don't teach like John McArthur. Or why I don't say things the way Billy Graham says them. The answer of course is simple. God didn't create me to be Chuck Swindoll, John McArthur, Billy Graham or anyone else. He created me to be me. He created you to be you. And my true uniqueness and your true uniqueness absolutely abolishes the need for competition between us.

So the first true thing God says about you is that you are special. You have great value because He made you in His image and you are completely unique.

Remember Who Loves You

Right now, can you name someone who really loves you? Even if you cannot name anyone, remember that God says you are loved. And we take Him at His word.

Research has shown that a tiny baby will actually give up the will to live and will die if all love is withheld. We each crave to be loved by our parents, by our children, by our friends—at work and in our neighborhood.

Not long ago the father of rock star Marvin Gaye shot and killed him. Friends of the artist whose music had gone to the top of the charts say he could have had anything he wanted. But a few weeks before his death Gaye had told them that all he ever wanted was his father's love.

I grew up in a small town in Michigan without really knowing how to give or receive love. My first model of love was not my parents. They didn't love each other; they merely had an existence together. I can never recall my father hugging my mother...or me.

Most people think from reading my first book, *Evidence That Demands A Verdict*, that I became a Christian because I could not intellectually refute Christianity. What most people don't know is that God used the intellectual challenge simply to open the door of my heart to His love. He got my attention through apologetics—the solid intellectual evidence supporting Christianity. But it was His love that broke down my resistance.

In the book of Jeremiah God says, "I have loved you with an everlasting love, with tender kindness I have drawn you" (Jeremiah 31:3). It was the love of God that turned me to Him. "For God so loved the world, that He gave His only begotten Son..." (John 3:16).

But, you say, that's past tense. What about right now? In the same book, Jesus says that the Father loves us—present tense. And in Romans 8, Paul documents God's love forever in the future, no matter what trials and hardships come our way, when he states that nothing can separate you or me from the love of God (verses 38,39).

A lot of people don't realize that God loved them even before they became Christians. In Romans 5, we learn that even when we were His enemies God loved us—even when we were still sinners (verse 8). If He loved us in that condition, how much more does He love us now as His adopted children? The depth of this love is revealed in John 15:9 when Jesus says, "Just as the Father has loved me, so have I loved you. Abide in my love."

Bill and Gloria Gaither wrote a song I have heard a number of times entitled "I Am Loved." One day a phrase in this song seemed to jump out at me: "I am loved. I am loved... *the One who knows me best loves me most*"[2] (italics mine). And it is true. Psalm 139 reveals that even before there is a word upon my lips, God knows it (verse

4). Yet this God who knows me better than my wife or anyone else in the world; this same God who knows you and me best, loves us most.

Dottie, my wife, was very fortunate in that she grew up with her parents' unconditional love and acceptance as a model of God's unconditional love. She says, "One reason I came to accept myself was because my parents loved me unconditionally. I knew that they loved me. I knew I was cherished. I knew that I delighted my parents and that they were proud of me. They would brag about me in the most healthy of ways and they could hardly wait to be with me. I was simply appreciated as the person that I was.

"When you have people who appreciate you and who think you're incredible, no matter what you do, it guides you when you are wrong and helps you develop a good self-image. My parents supported me in my uniqueness. They always told me that they loved me no matter what I did—matter how good or poor, for example, my grades might be. I never had even a shadow of doubt that they would always love me. Nor do I now. I don't think there is anything I could do that would ever turn off their love. That was the kind of love that I grew up with."

Accepting Your Acceptance

If you have ever experienced rejection, let me also assure you that *you are accepted*. In fact, you are accepted in the "Beloved."

We all long to be accepted just the way we are—at home, work or church. Actually, much of our energy is expended in trying to be accepted. I was helped a great deal by the realization that because of what Jesus Christ has done on the cross in taking away the penalty for my sins, God can accept me just the way I am. If I could have done anything to merit His acceptance, then my salvation would not be completely by faith. On the marvelous merit of Jesus Christ alone, God accepts you and me exactly the way we are. You can't improve on it.

But if you are like I was, you're having trouble believing that God truly accepts you. Even though I knew God accepted me because of the work of Jesus Christ on the cross in my behalf, I couldn't accept myself. And if I couldn't accept myself, how could I possibly trust anyone else to accept me? God, a marriage partner, anyone—all would obviously reject me as well. When I can't accept myself, a wall inevitably develops around the real me.

I discovered I was being hindered by two common fallacies about acceptance. Maybe they are sabotaging your self-image as well. One is that I thought I had to *be perfect*. Not only that, I thought I had to be *the best*.

It seems absurd now, but I really did set out to achieve perfection. I tried so hard to be an achiever. I once planned, down to the minute no less, my entire life and what I was going to accomplish. Why?

Because I thought the only sure way I could become accepted was to prove to myself and to everyone else that I *was* somebody. Deep inside I didn't really believe I had intrinsic worth.

With the hope that some of what I've experienced might help you see yourself more like God sees you, and to avoid the mistakes I've made, let me be very personal with you.

A lot of people wonder whether the popularity of my books and films, and the fact that I have spoken to more university students than anyone else alive, ever goes to my head. The truth is, I don't think so. And that's because I'm so aware that it is God who is working all this through me. One glance at my background reveals why I think of myself as the least likely person ever to be doing what I am doing.

Left-Handed Grace

You see, my folks never went beyond the second grade. I went to a little school in Michigan where my teachers taught grammar, but I didn't learn it, from them or from my parents. My grammar remained extremely poor. The closest I came to learning anything about speech was from my brother Jim. He was two years older than me—a sharp guy—and I used to dread his coming home from Michigan State, because every time he came home he would begin correcting my grammar.

I grew fearful of even opening my mouth around Jim. I'd say, "I don't want none of that." He would say, "Don't use a double negative." And I would tell him I didn't know "what no double negative" was.

My second grade teacher tried to switch me from being left-handed to right-handed, although I still don't mind being left-handed. (After all, the Bible says that Jesus is sitting on God's right hand. So God must be left-handed. And furthermore, research shows that you use the side of your brain opposite the hand you use, which means that "lefties" are the only ones who are in their "right mind".)

I don't know how the schools approach left-handedness today. Back then, I would have to go into a room with this teacher to practice being right-handed, two afternoons per week, while my friends were out playing softball and basketball. She would give me various tasks to do or things to build. Whenever I started to use my left hand she would reach over with a twelve-inch ruler and... WHACK! Of course, I would immediately withdraw my hand.

People laugh at this, but as a result of that treatment I developed a speech impediment. Whenever I felt tired, nervous, or scared, I would begin to stutter. I can remember having to get up and recite the Gettysburg Address at one point. I just stood there in front of the class, stammering, and the teacher kept repeating, "Say it! Say it!" I finally broke down crying in front of all my friends and ran out. It was a less-than-memorable start for a lifetime of public speaking. Not only that—

they informed all the other teachers about it.

The real problem was that no one ever told me they were trying to help me. I was left to believe that being left-handed proved I was inferior, or something even worse. In spite of the assumption, I remained determined they weren't going to change me. And they didn't.

My self-image problems didn't end, however, with grade school. In my first year at university an English professor was taking roll and asked about a classmate of mine. I blurted out, "He doesn't feel good today!" The professor immediately mocked me, "Mr. McDowell. He doesn't feel *well* today?" That was about the last time I spoke up in class. So, you can see why I believe I was a most unlikely candidate to be doing what I am doing today.

When Dr. Hampton, my college freshman counselor, looked over my records she observed, "Josh, you're a straight 'D' student. But you've got something that a lot of other people don't have."

"What's that?" I asked, "I'll take anything right now."

"You've got determination and drive," she said. "And that can take you further than most people's minds will ever take them. If you're willing to work at it, I'll be willing to work with you."

I seized the opportunity and spent hour upon hour recording tapes so that she could listen to them to correct my speech. And even though I felt a twinge of resentment every time I was corrected—sort of a "who do you think you are" feeling—I knew I was being helped. So I stuck with it.

My low sense of self-worth was regularly reinforced at my home church, at college, and at camp meetings. The challenge to commitment went something like this: "Bring your abilities, your talents, and give them to Jesus. He wants to take and to use you." I never went forward. And even after I had come to know Jesus Christ as Savior and Lord, I didn't believe the challenge applied to me. You see, I didn't think I had any abilities or assets. Of course I did, but as Proverbs reminds us, "As a man thinketh in his heart, so he is." I thought I had nothing going for me, and that is how I lived.

Bringing God Nothing

During the fall semester of my final year as an undergraduate at Wheaton College I heard a message by Dr. Richard Halverson, now chaplain of the U.S. Senate. He was speaking the last night of Spiritual Emphasis Week, and the auditorium was packed. When the invitation came, I thought, *Here we go again.* "Bring your talents, your abilities, your gifts and place them on the alter and say, 'God, here I am. Use me.'"

Hundreds of students did respond. As I sat there wondering why I should have to endure this again, I suddenly stood up, right in front of everyone, and burst out the side door into the night air. I ran all the way to the dorm and tried to go to sleep, but I couldn't. Later I roused Chaplain Walsh out of bed, but that didn't help. I called the young lady I was engaged to. She couldn't help either.

At about four o'clock in the morning I found myself walking down West Union Street in Wheaton, Illinois. A "hunter's moon"—the full moon of October—lit up the night. I had reached the end of my proverbial rope, and I just cried out, "God, I've had it." I don't know if my words and attitudes were exactly right or not, but I said, "God, I don't think I have any strengths. I don't think I have any abilities. I stutter. I've got bad grammar. I can't do this and I can't do that. But here they are—all my limitations and all my shortcomings. Here are my weaknesses. I give them to You. If You can take them and glorify Yourself, I'll serve You for the rest of my life with every breath I have."

Ever since that desperate prayer I have been different—living life on a supernatural level. Because of the indwelling presence of His Holy Spirit, God truly has taken my shortcomings and turned them into my strongest assets.

Too many people feel sorry for themselves because of some weak area in their lives. They are convinced that God can't use them because of it. I am living proof that God uses people who aren't perfect. God is greater than your limitations. And when Christians will simply stop moping around in self-pity and begin honestly presenting themselves to the Lord, they will discover that Jesus Christ will meet them, right where they are. He will develop them into His image.

I believe that when you are enjoying a healthy self-image and seeing yourself as God sees you—no more and no less—then you can face your limitations. You can yield them to Christ to work on—and at the same time you can yield your abilities and strengths so that they won't lead to pride in your life. You do not have to be perfect to have a healthy self-image. You simply need to celebrate the unique person that God made you to be.

I often walk around imagining a sign on my back which reads, "Still under construction." I have learned to accept myself on the same basis as God accepts me—through Jesus Christ and His death on the cross. It took years for me to realize this as a Christian. But once I saw that I could accept myself, I became free to accept other people just the way they are, without putting conditions on those relationships.

God's love, you see, is unconditional and His acceptance is unconditional. He accepts you right now just the way you are. This is why John wrote, "In this is love, not that we loved God, but that He loved us and sent His Son to be the propitiation for our sins" (1 John 4:10). God accepts you because He has forgiven you on the basis of what Jesus Christ did on your behalf. I no longer believe that first fallacy, that *I have to be perfect* to be acceptable. I am perfect in Jesus Christ, and that's all the acceptance I really need.

My Best Is Enough!

The second fallacy about self-acceptance that haunted me was that I thought I had to *be the best* to be acceptable. I meet so many people who think they have to be the best cook in the whole world, the best businessman in the state, or the best tackle in the NFL. They are driven by this in order to accept themselves and to feel accepted by others. The problem is, of course, that if you have to be the best at what you do to accept yourself, then only one musician, one student and one salesman in the entire country will ever accept himself or herself.

A rookie major league pitcher was once asked, "What's wrong?" He replied, "The first batter I faced today started playing with the Red Sox when I was in fourth grade. On the first pitch I threw him the hardest fastball of my life."

"What happened?"

"He spit on it as it went by!"

This rookie was in trouble. His self-image depended on the situation. In the minors he had been a big shot. The batters considered him a tough pitcher. Yet with a quick change of uniforms, moving from minor to major league, his fearsome fastball had fizzled, and his self-image along with it.

If that's the way we are going to live (and most of us do), then we are faced with having to be the very best at everything, all of the time, in order to be satisfied with ourselves. And while we all do well in some areas, we all fall short in others. So if we are dependent upon our situation we are inevitably left struggling with our self-image.

Could this be how God wants us to live? Certainly not! The apostle Paul says, "Let everyone be sure that he is doing the very best." Why? "Because you have the satisfaction of a job well done and there is no need to compare yourself with someone else" (Galations 6:4 TLB). God's love and acceptance of us does not require special circumstances, and this is the view He wants us to have of ourselves.

If I go to speak at a conference, and I've done my best with the talents and abilities that God has given me through the power of His Holy Spirit, then I don't care if there are fifty other speakers there that are better than I am. I can go back to the motel room, look in the mirror and say, "McDowell, you're cool! I like you! You took what was given to you and did your best to the glory of God." When one has a healthy self-image, you can do that. It's when I don't do my best with the things that are important that I'm not satisfied with myself.

But what is our standard for determining what is important? Is it what God says that is important? What your family says? Your friends? Or you? We must not forget that there are many situations in life in which doing our best isn't important. Some people may want to do their best at cooking, which is fine by me, especially when they have me over for dinner. But if they do put their very best effort into every breakfast, lunch, dinner and snack, they will burn out on cooking before long. We must put our best only into what really requires it.

I was helped to accept this by remembering that God loves me... *just the way I am.* When I came to Jesus Christ and placed my trust in Him as Savior and Lord, I realized from clear biblical teaching that God loved and accepted me just the way I was. With all my shortcoming, with all my faults, God accepted me. Logically then, this is the foundation for my accepting myself.

When you simply *do* your best, you're not in competition with anyone else and you are free to appreciate yourself as God made you. C. S. Lewis says in *The Screwtape Letters* that God wants man "in the end, to be so free from any bias in his own favor that he can rejoice in his own talents as frankly and gratefully as his neighbor's talents—or in a sunrise, an elephant, or a waterfall. He wants each man, in the long run, to be able to recognize all creatures (even himself) as glorious and excellent things."[3]

This realization also opened the door for me up to accept others. I don't have to put them on a performance basis where they have to prove themselves to me. I can accept them, just as God accepts me. Because I can accept myself, Josh McDowell, the way I am, I am able to trust my wife, Dottie, to accept me the way I am. Therefore, I can open myself to her and be truly free in my conversations and actions.

Loving With Real Love

Another way of having a healthy self-image—seeing yourself as God sees you—is being a channel of love. One of the greatest needs in the church today is for believers to demonstrate divine love for each other and to the world around them.

On a television show once I debated for three and a half hours with the co-founder of *Playboy*. He was a situational ethicist and believed there is no right or wrong, that in every situation the circumstances will dictate what one ought to do. In other words, before you enter a situation there is no right or wrong, but once you're there, you are to do "the loving thing—what seems right to do."

Adherents of this philosophy quote Romans 13:8, which says, "Owe no man anything except to love one another; for he who loves his neighbor has fulfilled the law." However, they never go on to verse 9 where Paul writes, "Thou shalt not commit murder. Thou shalt not steal. Thou shalt not covet."

What does this mean? It means that a loving God gave us commandments. He gave us various admonitions throughout the Bible to give our loving actions solid content, so that when He says, "Love one another," I can know what is the loving thing to do. If you truly love someone, you won't murder or steal from them.

When someone tells me, "Well, the person said if I really loved them I'd have sex with them," if it's outside the commitment of marriage, I can honestly say that if you really loved that person, then you wouldn't. That wouldn't be loving with real love. God didn't command you and me to love one another and then leave it for us to arbitrarily invent definitions of love to suit the moment. He has given content to that love. He defined loving for us in 1 Corinthians 13, in the Ten Commandments in Exodus 20, and throughout the Bible.

One of the most memorable examples I have encountered of being a love channel because of one's secure sense of self-identity was shown by an Eastern Airlines stewardess. Over the past eighteen years I have boarded close to 5,000 flights, so I have experienced just about everything that can happen on an airplane. But I had never seen what greeted me on a flight from Atlanta to Chicago. As I moved through first class on my way back to the "cattle car," a stewardess was standing there welcoming everyone with a big smile and holding a dozen roses.

That's unusual, I thought. And not being an introvert, I said as I walked by, "Your boyfriend bought you some flowers?" She said, "No." "Then who did?" I asked. She answered, "I did!" Isn't that weird? I didn't know what to say, so I found my seat and sat down.

I couldn't stop thinking about what she had said. It intrigued me so much that before the plane pushed back from the gate, I went back and introduced myself. Discovering she was a Christian, I said, "Could I ask you a very personal question? Why did you buy yourself a dozen roses?"

"Because I like myself," she answered.

Think of that! Because she liked herself she went out and bought herself a dozen roses.

The Eloquence of Flowers

Now let me ask you, have you ever bought yourself a dozen roses? Over the years I have spent some lonely nights away from home; away from my wife; away from my two daughters and my son. As a staff speaker with Campus Crusade for Christ, the loneliest night of the year is probably New Year's Eve. I leave home Christmas night or the next morning and travel around the United States speaking at several Christmas conferences. I speak all day, then travel at night. Then I speak the next day and travel again and so forth, usually ending up on New Year's Eve afternoon in San Jose, California.

For thirteen out of the last fourteen years, after it's all over I have flown to John Wayne Airport in Orange County, where someone picks me up and takes me to the same hotel I have stayed in, on the same beach, each year. My wife and children are in Boston with her parents. I am physically, emotionally and spiritually exhausted, and I rest.

A few years ago after my speaking tour again ended, Don Stewart, who has written several books with me, picked me up in his little Honda Civic at John Wayne Airport and we headed down the freeway. Just as we came into Laguna Beach, we passed a flatbed truck loaded with flowers. I asked Don to stop and he did—right in the middle of the road. I asked him to pull over to the curb, and I got out and went over to the truck and bought five dozen flowers.

Have you ever tried to get into a Honda Civic with five dozen flowers? It's not easy—especially if no one opens the door for you. I stood there with all those flowers and Don just looked at me without saying a word. He told me later that he was thinking: "Here's Josh McDowell, on staff with Campus Crusade for Christ, Christian speaker, his wife is in Boston, it's New Year's Eve and he's going to a hotel room with five dozen flowers. That's rumor material."

He didn't say anything for a while, but as we drove down Pacific Coast Highway he finally blurted out, "Why did you buy the flowers?" I wanted to say, "It's none of your business," but I didn't. I told him that I was tired, and when I get this way Satan likes to work in my life. He likes to discourage me, to get my eyes off God, off the victories and onto the problems.

I said, "Don, I'm going to be here for four days and I'm going to put these flowers all over my room. I'm going to put one dozen on the balcony, another dozen on the TV, another dozen I'll put on the table by the bed. And every time I look at a dozen flowers it's going to be God saying to me, 'Josh, I love you. Josh, I accept you. Josh, I forgive you. Josh, as the Father has loved Me so have I loved you. Josh, you are special!' I'll look at each dozen flowers and hear God saying, 'Josh, you're of great value, I created you in My image. Josh, you're unique.'" You know—I have never been able to look at flowers the same way since that New Years.

So I ask you again, have you bought yourself a dozen roses? To know the secret of loving—to have a maximum love, marriage and sex relationship—you must be the right person. And the first ingredient this requires is having a healthy self-image. It's available! The genuine self-image God created for you is yours if you're willing to believe it and to receive it.

Questions to Ponder

- What do you like about the way God made you?
- In what way are you a unique person?
- How do you know God has accepted you?
- What can you do today or tomorrow to be a channel of love?

FURTHER HELPFUL RESOURCES:
Bruce Narramore, *You're Someone Special* (Zondervan)
Verna Birkey, *You Are Very Special* (Fleming H. Revell)

4

KEEP CLEAR CHANNELS

Have you ever stopped to consider what you bring to a relationship as a natural result of who you are? What did your partner bring?

You see, when two individuals come together in a relationship, and especially in the commitment of marriage, they each bring a unique background, culture and style of communication. Two different life styles, catalogues of experience and personal histories are being blended into a single unit. Unless each has strong communication skills and is able to understand the other person, there can never be satisfying intimacy. The ability to communicate consistently at meaningful levels is one of the most fundamental requirements of being the right person.

Inability to communicate is the most common marital complaint heard by both psychologists and marital therapists today. In a survey of 730 professional marriage counselors, it was reported by an overwhelming majority that the marital problem they treated most frequently was a "breakdown in communication."[1]

The *Ladies Home Journal* polled over 30,000 women and only one problem ranked above conflicts over money, "poor communication." Researcher Terri Schultz writes that, "Although many women chose their partners based on sex appeal, research shows that if they had to do it again, they said the ability to communicate is much more important."[2] For these now wiser women the ability to communicate in a relationship ranked higher than sexual attraction, physical appearance and personality.

Research documents that vital, fulfilled marriages are enjoyed by those couples who share their feelings and who have a greater amount of openness with their spouses. The chief dysfunction in failing marriages is not sexual. It is verbal.

Dr. Mark Lee quotes studies in eleven countries which "show that the happiest couples are the ones that talk the most to each other." As a marriage counselor, Lee notes that the "emerging problem in marriage is alienation. We know that the average couple, after one year of marriage, spends thirty-seven minutes a week in meaningful, private conversation—by far too little."[3]

In an exclusive interview, lawyer Herbert A. Glieberman, a renowned specialist in divorce and family law for twenty-eight years, was asked to name the single biggest reason couples split up. Glieberman replied, "Number one is the inability to talk honestly with each other—to bare their souls and treat each other as their best friend...I find too many people talk right through each other rather than to each other...."[4]

Leo Buscaglia sent marriage questionnaires to one thousand people and told *USA Today* that "at least eighty-five percent of the respondents said the most important quality to keep this thing going is communication—the ability for two people to talk to each other on a real gut level."[5]

Lynn Atwater, a sociologist on the faculty of Seton Hall University, says that women have extramarital affairs mainly because they want deeper emotional intimacy. She points to new reseach which reveals that women regard physical pleasure and variety as important, but unlike men, don't seek affairs mainly for the sex. "Men are always asking me what they can do to prevent their wives from having an affair," says Atwater. "I advise, 'Talk to her.'" According to Atwater, women regard emotional communication to be the greatest reward of an affair.[6]

Communication is simply the principle way we learn more about each another. The greater one's capacity is to really communicate, the deeper the satisfaction both partners can experience in the relationship. Two people living in close proximity will surface differences. If these differences are not talked over, they inevitably lead to confusion and conflict. Even the apostle Paul and his associate, Barnabas, experienced this. Apparently they had not ever discussed how they felt about the defection of John Mark—until the time arrived for a second trip. Then it proved to be too late to get agreement.

A Verbal Intercourse

What does it mean to communicate? According to the *Random House Dictionary* it means "to give or interchange thoughts, feelings, information, or the like, by writing, speaking, etc." Dr. H. Norman Wright, a marriage counselor and the author of numerous excellent books on family communication, offers this simple definition: "Communication is a process (either verbal or nonverbal) of sharing information with another person in such a way that he understands what you are saying. *'Talking'* and *'listening'* and *'understanding'* are all involved in the process of communication."[7]

Communication means truly sharing yourself with one another. This dialogue is *the vital need* of couples today.

"Dialogue takes place," writes Dwight Small, "when two people communicate the full meaning of their lives to one another, when they participate in each other's lives in the most meaningful ways in which they are capable."[8]

"It takes two partners to communicate," says Cynthia Deutsch in her article, "The Danger of the Silent Partner." "If one partner is unwilling, there can be talk, but no communication. Communicating about problems is a difficult activity and one that makes people feel vulnerable. Yet no relationship exists without some problems, and discussing them is the way to go about resolving them. If one partner does not participate, there will be no resolution, and the problem at issue can intensify and spread to other areas of the relationship. This can be especially true if it is the same partner who persistently and consistently refuses to discuss certain issues."

Deutsch adds, "When one partner refuses communication, the strong tendency is for the other to begin refusing to give in the relationship as well, and in what can be a very short time, the partners can become angry, feel rejected, and become alienated from each other. Often even after the central issue is resolved, the other areas of interaction must be rebuilt as well. Good communication, which opens people to each other, can be very fragile, and once it is broken it requires careful and often painstaking repairs."[9]

Most people think of talking as communication—with the goal of getting their point of view across. Meaningful communication, however, is twofold—both talking *and* listening. The facet most neglected by couples today is listening.

From the fact that God gave us two ears and one mouth, the Irish have drawn the thoughtful conclusion that we should listen twice as much as we talk. James wrote, "Be quick to hear, slow to speak" (James 1:19), and Shakespeare echoed the dictum in these words, "Give every man thy ear, but few thy voice."[10]

The phrase "quick to hear" means to be "a ready listener." But most people are a lot more comfortable in communication when they are doing the talking. They feel greater security in asserting their own position, feelings, opinions and ideas than in listening to those of another. Listening is the most difficult aspect of communication for most people. Listening never comes naturally.

Extroverts Beware!

When one or the other in a relationship lacks the ability to listen effectively, frustrations set in which will mature into serious relational problems if not dealt with. Extroverts (like me) are often especially guilty of talking too much and not listening enough. It's a problem that I'm still working on in my marriage.

About seven or eight months after Dottie and I were married, she came to me rather hesitantly. I could tell she was hurting. "I don't think you love me," she confessed.

"What?" I exclaimed, "You've got to be kidding! I love you more than anyone else on the face of this earth."

"Honey," she replied, "I really don't think you are interested in some of the areas of my life that interest me. I don't think you care about some of the 'little' areas."

Ouch! That was like driving a knife through my heart. Immediately I asserted, "But I do too!"

I was amazed as Dottie explained why she felt that way. "You never listen to me. I will start to share something with you and you will cut me off or change the subject. Or, I will start to share something with you and your mind is off somewhere else. You often pretend you're listening, but your mind is on a free-speech platform in Bolivia." That's my wife's way of saying, "Darling, you're thinking about something else while I'm talking to you."

One indicator of a healthy relationship is the number of little phrases that emerge that are meaningful only to the couple. I won't share all of the ones Dottie and I have, but when she wants me to know that I'm looking at her, but thinking of something else, she'll say, "You're on a free-speech platform in Bolivia!" (I got my start doing free-speech debates with Marxists in Latin America.)

You know what I discovered was happening? Because I had never learned to listen to people, I was unintentionally communicating to my wife that I didn't care. She was starting to retreat into a shell.

"Attention to what our mate says," writes Richard Austin, "is one measure of our respect. Too often we hear the words of a conversation but do not really hear the message. Listening to words and hearing the message are quite different."[11]

Since I had not made a concerted effort (and sometimes no effort at all) to listen to Dottie, I was communicating to her that what she had to say wasn't important to me. What a way to strangle a partner's enthusiasm! Really listening says to another person, "You are important! You are of great value!" Respect begins with listening.

Listening is one of the most profound ways to show someone that you take them seriously; that you care; that you value their opinion. Dr. David Augsburger puts it this way, "An open ear is the only believable sign of an open heart."[12] Here's how Augsburger relates effective listening to a person's self-esteem:

"If you listen to me, then I must be worth hearing.

"If you ignore me, I must be a bore.

"If you approve of my views or values, then I have something of worth to offer.

"If you disapprove of my comment or contribution, then I apparently had nothing to say.

"If I cannot be with you without using your comments for self-evaluation, then leveling will be impossible. If I am preoccupied with what you think of me, then I have already shut you out."[13]

Beyond Mere Listening

Have you ever said to your mate, "You're not listening," only to have him say, "Oh yes I am," and then repeat the last sentence to you? If so, you recognize it is one thing to *hear* and quite another to *listen*. As Dr. Norman Wright describes the difference: "Hearing is basically to gain content or information for your own purposes. Listening is caring for and being empathetic toward the person who is talking....Hearing means that you are concerned about what is going on inside you during the conversation. Listening means that you are trying to understand the feelings of the other person and are listening for his sake."[14]

The biblical concept of hearing is not a reference merely to audio sounds; it also means "to pay heed." And the value of a listening ear has been confirmed again by sociologists George Warheit and Charles Holzer III from the University of Florida. They "have done research that indicates that the availablility of one's friends and family has more to do with vulnerability to depression than even the number or kind of stressful experiences you suffer. The study showed that even people who were under a great deal of stress were able to cope with that stress better when they had close human contacts. As you might guess, the study showed that those without a husband or wife seemed most susceptible to depression."[15]

There are various levels of listening. And Dr. Augsburger relates each level to *caring* in his book, *Caring Enough to Hear and Be Heard*: "One can listen for facts, data, detail to use for one's own ends or to quote for other purposes, and so offer no caring at all.

"Or one can listen out of sympathy that is energized by pity. To be nourished by one's own pitying is to feed one's pride on the pain of others. To be moved by pity to care is a far different thing. Simple sympathy may not be caring at all.

"Or one can listen as another ventilates about a person not present and actually increase the pain and distance between them by implying, through listening, that gossiping about absent others is useful talk. It's not caring at all.

"Or one can listen out of apathy or obligation or professional habit or simple niceness, and give no real caring to the other. To care is more than to offer an ear. Habitual hearing may not be caring after all.

"Or one can listen inquisitively, with the curiosity of a voyeur peering in at another's private zones. To care is more than to offer wide eyes. The eager ear or eye may not care at all.

"Or one can listen 'helpfully' as a rescuer with ready first aid, inserting support, understanding, reassurance at each pause. To care is to both give and withhold help. Being chronically helpful may be no help at all.

"Yet caring includes elements of each of the above. Accurate attention to what is said, a genuine empathy, a willingness to stand with another when he or she is saying things that are exaggerated through stress, a disinterest that allows objectivity, a willingness to see the other as he or she is, a commitment to be truly helpful as the moment for useful help arrives—all these are ingredients in real care, but they are each clarified and corrected by the central element of caring."[16]

Now when one fails to listen to one's mate it doesn't always lead to silence. In many situations it can result in increased talking. Joyce Landorf, a perceptive author in the area of relationships, explains why some people become compulsive talkers. She asks men whose wives are constantly talking: "Was she always that way, even before you were married? Or did she just seem to get that way with time? Some women talk at the moment of birth and a steady stream follows each moment of their lives forever after, but others have developed a nonstop flow of talk for other reasons.

"Many times a compulsive talker is really shouting to be heard by someone. The more bored you look, the more you yawn, the more you watch the dog or TV, the harder she talks. She just talks all the more to compensate. You may have stopped listening to her a long time ago, and she knows that better than anybody.

"Do you think this has happened to you? When was the last time that you asked these questions of your wife: 'How do you feel about...?' and/or 'What happened at home today?' Do you ever intersperse her remarks with, 'You may be right, Hon.' If your wife feels you are not willing to listen to her, she has two options: to talk louder and harder; or to talk less and withdraw. Either way, it's very hard on the marriage."[17]

It is imperative that we recognize that we always communicate in one way or another. In other words, even silence is communication. So, the key is to do it effectively, in a way that creates a climate of greater intimacy and vulnerability. But, before we look at some ways to improve our ability to listen, let's look at another facet of effective communication.

Talking—More or Less

Talking is the second ingredient of communication. Most people need to improve in one or the other—listening or talking. But then there are those, like myself, who need to grow in both areas because of peculiarities in our personal styles.

Dottie delights in sharing details and she needs to hear details. I don't. I just want the big picture. As a result, for a long time there was frustration in our relationship because I didn't understand her need to communicate details.

One day Dottie said to me, "Honey, you don't talk right." I said, "I've talked like this my whole life!" She said, "Well, we're not communicating." I asked her what she meant, and she replied that I never shared any details—I never let her know what was really happening. Then she gave me an illustration. After a very important conference she would ask me how the meetings went and I would just say, "Oh, very well," and then go on to something else. She knew that there had to be more to it than that, and it was those details that she wanted to hear.

Another example of the detail she needs to hear would surface when I would mention that some friends of ours had given birth to a baby. "When?" she would ask. "I don't know," I would reply. "How much did it weigh?" Again, I wouldn't know. "Was it a boy or a girl?" "Beats me," I would say. "What did they name it?" she would ask and so on. I was satisfied with what I knew, but I certainly wasn't able to communicate adequately with my wife.

"Think details!" became my motto. I started writing myself notes: "Josh, when you talk with your mate you need to bring in details." (And it has produced positive results in other relationships also.) Now I can hardly wait to talk to my wife after a friend has delivered a baby. "When?" "Last Tuesday." "How much did it weigh?" "8 pounds." "Was it a boy or a girl?" "A boy." "What did they name him?" "Jim," and so forth. I *do* remember things that I never bothered with before, and it has enhanced our marital communication because I am able to give Dottie the details—a strong channel through which she can feel my love.

For some of us it's details. For others the need may be to share feelings with the other person—to let them know what's going on inside. This area has also troubled me. I find it easy to talk on a wide range of subjects, and even though I know the importance to a relationship of sharing my innermost thoughts, it's still difficult for me.

This is why we tend to talk about subjects that don't really matter—the weather, how we feel physically, and so on. Few of us readily share our ideas or opinions with others when they involve our innermost thoughts and feelings. Yet the intimacy this sort of communication produces is absolutely crucial to enjoying a healthy love and marriage relationship.

You may be asking, "How can I become a better communicator? A better listener? A better talker?" I want to suggest to you and anyone you love, some practical ways you can improve your skills at interpersonal communications. These principles will increase the opportunity for knowing a greater depth of caring in your relationship.

If you're single, let these be a guide to enhancing your personal communication with others. Apply them immediately in your dating situations. If you are married, let these principles mirror your communication with your spouse (and children.) Most marriages can never develop intimacy beyond the level of your communication skills and your desire for openness and verbal intercourse with each other.

Questions to Ponder

- What are some of the special phrases that express how you feel about your mate?
- What kind of a listener are you? Ask your mate to describe the way you listen.
- When will you and your spouse take quality time to improve your comminication?

5

BECOMING A BETTER COMMUNICATOR

By now you may be saying, "Hey, I know I've got a problem. Tell me what I can do about it. How can I build a more loving relationship by better communication?"

Eleven principles have helped me through the years as I worked at becoming a better communicator. I don't expect you to memorize them or be able to implement them immediately. Yet you may want to read this chapter several times, or even copy down the principles themselves so you can hang them over a desk or a sink.

If you are a single, the following principles will enhance your personal communication with others in your circle of friends. If you are dating, you will certainly want to apply them immediately.

For those of you who are married, these principles can dramatically improve your communication with your spouse and children. Most marriages do not ever develop intimacy beyond the level of communication between spouses—and that, of course, depends on how much you desire openness and verbal intercourse. Should you be a parent, effective implementation of these principles will reduce the complaint, "You aren't listening to me" (probably the biggest complaint teens have against their parents).

Ready for some action? Here are the ten principles:

1. Work at it.
2. Learn to compromise.
3. Seek to understand.
4. Affirm your spouse's worth, dignity and value.

5. Be positive and encouraging.
6. Practice confidentiality.
7. Wait for the right time.
8. Share your feelings.
9. Avoid mind-reading.
10. Give a response.
11. Be honest.

Now that they are on the table, let's see how they work out in everyday life. Dottie will be joining me again so you'll see how we are working at implementing these principles.

1. Work at It

Doing what comes naturally may be the motto for many in our culture, but becoming a good communicator does not just happen. All of us have been twisted by the self-centeredness of our lives, so we need to make a lot of effort based on solid commitment to better communication. God does not just wave a magic wand over us after we enter into a personal relationship with Him. Instead, He gives us the will and the desire, and then helps us do it if we get moving.

My philosophy is that if you want someone to know that you are bleeding, you've got to hemorrhage. With Dottie, I began going out of my way to listen to her, and to let her know that I was really interested in those areas that she found important. It did not come naturally—I had to work at it.

One of my habits was to read the newspaper at breakfast. I continued it early into our marriage. When Dottie, however, reminded me that the breakfast table is a great place to talk, I gave it up. For the past ten years of our marriage I cannot remember ever reading a newspaper at the breakfast table. I've learned to cue myself as I walk to the table, "Now, Josh, remember. You're going to listen to your wife."

When Dottie came into my study I used to say, "Honey, I can't right now. I'm busy." But working at making communication with her a priority requires a different response. Now when she comes in, no matter what I'm doing, I stop, turn toward her and try my best to concentrate on what she says. For me, developing the habit even required saying to myself, "I am going to *hear everything* my wife says and I am going to respond to everything my wife says."

On the road, I'm quite sensitive to the cost of calling home. But I began to realize that it's even harder for the one at home than for the partner who is traveling. Dottie may have waited all day to share something with me—something that happened at home that she wanted to talk about—and I'd say, "This is long distance. Tell me when I get home."

This response shredded Dottie's motivation to open up and communicate. So I've had to learn to prepare myself by saying, "Josh, when Dottie answers, you are not going to take care of business first. You are going to say, 'What's been happening today?' and then listen eagerly as she expresses her views and talks about her needs." The calls cost me more now, but it's some of the best money I have ever invested.

One day as I came through the door from a trip Dottie threw her arms around me and said, "Honey, thank you so much!" I said, "For what?" "For listening to me," she said. I had really been concentrating on listening and it has paid off in every area of our relationship. Dottie now *knows* that what she has to say is important to me.

If you want to become someone worth marrying, among other things you must develop the skill of being a good listener and that takes work. I only wish someone had given me advice like this years ago.

2. Learn to Compromise

A healthy marriage relationship is a give-and-take situation, especially where differing styles of communicating are involved. Each person needs the freedom to be himself or herself while still adapting to the other's needs. One style isn't necessarily better than another. It's just that people are different when it comes to needs in communication and a skillful communicator knows when to adjust.

Dottie and I have opposite needs for sharing details. Perhaps you can identify with the frequent frustration that can spawn. As Dottie puts it, "Josh likes to get right to the point. He likes to know his facts. He wants the bottom line. I've been told I have a flair for the dramatic. Because of my personality I think telling a story should be a work of art—much like painting a picture. You don't approach an easel with a paint roller. You apply the details one at a time. So when telling a story, I don't really try to be dramatic. I just think there's a stage to be set, a tone to be developed and an atmosphere to be communicated.

"When Josh and I were first married I think my style of communicating nearly drove him 'to the moon.' His body language would be screaming, 'Just get to the point!' And he would finally say, 'What's the point of the story?' And I would respond, 'Look, you're going to have to listen to this my way. It's my story.' Eventually he began to realize that details in a story are very important to me.

"I've also come to realize the essential place of compromise in a marriage. I think we both now try to work at meeting each other's needs. He tries to remember more of the details and to be patient with me when I'm giving details. In turn, I try to spare him the agony of sitting through the extraneous. I try to summarize my message without the drama; to delete the feelings and get to the bottom line.

"We do have very different styles of communication, but together we're more effective. One's strength tends to balance out the other's. I've learned to adapt and Josh has learned to adapt. It's broadened our perspectives, and I think that is one of most significant aspects of two people coming together in marriage. You do things differently; you see things differently; you communicate differently.

"My pregnancy with our third child, Katie, is a good example. After we had Kelly and Sean we both knew we wanted another child, but I became pregnant with Katie a bit earlier than we had anticipated. Josh was traveling when I first suspected it. I knew he would be thrilled, but I didn't want to add stress to his incredible speaking schedule at that particular time. So I decided that rather than telling him over the phone I would wait until I knew for sure. I had to keep the whole thing to myself for a few days.

"To give Josh the news, I made up a real cute little poem that said in a roundabout way that I was pregnant. I wrote it in such a way that you had to listen all the way through to the very last line before you realized what it was getting at, and that it was about us.

"At the time we were living in Texas and still involved in buying and selling antiques. Josh was in California when all this was happening, and I happened to call him in San Bernardino just five minutes before a big antique sale was to start. I said, 'I need to talk to you,' and he said, 'Okay, that's fine, but I don't have much time. They're getting ready to open the door, and there are 500 people waiting to get in.' I told him I had something to read, and he agreed to listen as long as I read it fast.

"I started reading the poem and he interrupted me in the middle and said, 'Wait a minute, whose poem is this?' I told him to be quiet for a minute and just listen. Twice more he broke in as I was reading: 'Hold on, what are you talking about? Who is having a baby?' I just kept insisting, 'Don't say anything. You have to hear the whole poem.'

"Finally, at the end, he realized that I was telling him *we* were going to have a baby. Now Josh would rather I had just stated the fact: 'I'm pregnant. We're going to have a baby in June.' But *I* had to go around the block, paint this picture, set the atmosphere and make it very exciting. It drove him bananas. (Although I think he enjoyed it once it was over!) This was my way of communicating something very special, and I had to be me in doing it. For a few minutes it was difficult for him, but he listened and it meant a lot to me.

"There are many times when I adapt to his mindset and communicate quickly. At other times I say, 'You're going to have to listen to this whole thing, because I'm telling the story my way!' It's a give and take, and that's how marriage has to be. It's part of what makes it fun."

3. Seek to Understand

Have you ever agreed to meet someone at a specific building downtown, only to wait in vain while your friend looked for you half a block away? You thought you were very clear in your communication, but she did not understand it clearly.

Recently friends of mine took her parents to the Los Angeles airport. As they approached the airport, my friend said to his wife, "Should I drop the folks off at the departure level?" Busy watching traffic, he heard her say something about parking, and assumed she preferred to park first.

On the way in, she started pointing out the parking areas for the various terminals, so he took this as a further cue for her desire to park first. Yet when he headed the car into a parking spot she became quite indignant.

"Now we have to carry those heavy suitcases all that way into the terminal," she fumed.

After a bit of verbal jockeying, he realized the better part of valor was to leave the parking lot, circle and stop at the departure level—so that he could get the parents and baggage checked in while she parked the car. Only on the way out of the airport did he discover her reference to parking as they approached the airport had been the last word of a sentence: "After we drop them off I'll park the car." Because he had not taken the time to understand the full communication, he had totally misread her intentions.

A little placard I've frequently seen posted on office walls reads: "I know you believe you understand what you think I said. But I am not sure you realize that what you heard is not what I meant." One of the keys to communication and to developing intimacy is to realize that the other person is not only trying to understand, but he or she truly cares. This empathy will cause both individuals to be more open in the relationship.

When, on the other hand, you sense that the other person doesn't want to listen, or is not trying to understand you, it affects your self-esteem. You soon begin to withdraw because you feel that what you have to say is not being viewed as important. You start to feel that you are not important and the relationship moves toward a danger zone. Previous biases or negative expectations must be set on the shelf to keep them from distorting the conversation you are having. Our commitment must be to really hear the other person, regardless of differing convictions or disagreements.

"Acceptance," according to Dr. H. Norman Wright, "does not mean that you agree with the content of what is said. Rather, it means that you understand that what your spouse is saying is something that he/she feels." He adds that "sensitive listening is reaching out to the other person; actively caring about what he says and what he wants to say."[1]

The best commentary I've heard on Jesus' commandment to "love your neighbor as yourself" (Matt. 22:39) is by David Augsburger: "To love you as I love myself is to seek to hear you as I want to be heard and understand you as I long to be understood."² If each person had this as a motto to live out in relationships, our divorce lawyers would go out of business.

"Communication," observes Richard Strauss, "is the means by which we learn to know and understand our mates. God, however, already understands our mates; He created them. Let us ask Him to open our channels of interpersonal communication and give us the same understanding that He has; that our marriage relationship may grow increasingly precious every day."³

4. Affirm Your Spouse's Worth, Dignity, and Value

Every person has a deep need to be heard, to be *listened to*. The very act of listening communicates a sense of value, esteem, love and dignity. It makes the person feel important. And a relationship usually will not progress beyond the level of mutual communication and respect shown by each person, one for the other. Try always to reinforce the image of Christ.

George and Nikki Kochler explain the need for affirming value and esteem through careful listening: "When you and I listen to another person we are conveying the thought that 'I'm interested in you as a person, and I think that what you feel is important. I respect your thoughts, even if I don't agree with them. I know that they are valid for you. I feel sure that you have a contribution to make. I'm not trying to change you or evaluate you. I just want to understand you. I think you're worth listening to, and I want you to know that I'm the kind of person that you can talk to.' "⁴

A person with low or unhealthy self-esteem doesn't feel as though he or she has anything worthwhile to say. This person will have a fear of transparency because of possible rejection. Dottie tells me that one way she feels my love and esteem for her is when I praise her mind.

"He's always telling me what a quick mind I have and how bright I am, which, coming from Josh, is quite a compliment because I think he's so incredible.

"Another way he manifested his love was to fill in for me in my volunteer work at the elementary school. I serve as a classroom reading aid. But a few times last year, for one reason or another, I couldn't go and had to find somebody to fill in for me. So Josh went and taught the second graders how to read. It was just one more action that said to me, 'I'm interested in what you do, I love you, and I want to help you.'

"Also Josh tells me all the time how much he loves me and respects me and backs it up with his words and actions. He asks my opinion when he's editing books, films or lectures. He's always open to my opinions and doesn't just breeze by them. He likes to know how I feel about certain things and he values what I have to say. When I feel intuitively strong about something, he takes it seriously. His very actions communicate to me that he thinks I'm special."

I can assure you, this is not the "natural" me. Only as I became willing to make the effort to understand her, did this "fruit" appear.

5. Be Positive and Encouraging

Being positive is a real plus factor in communications. It promotes openness with your mate, whereas criticism tends to hinder healthy communications. Two very critical people may communicate, but it will not be healthy communication. By nature we each tend to accentuate and remember the negative.

During a three-day lecture series at the University of Tennessee, I was in a meeting with the Campus Crusade staff and several key students. One of the students walked in and said, "I'm not going to hand out any more fliers. Everybody's negative about the meetings. All I've heard is negative reports this morning."

I immediately asked, "How many people have given you a hard time? Twenty-five?"

"No."

"Ten?"

"No."

"Was it five?" I asked.

Again she said, "No."

We discovered only two people had reacted negatively to the two or three hundred fliers she had handed out. Everyone in the room, including her, realized that she had accentuated the negative.

In interpersonal communication we tend to notice or remember only the negative from conversations or statements about ourselves. Ten positive statements and one negative one may be made, but we will remember the negative one most. The ratio of praise to criticism in a conversation ought to be a healthy 90 percent praise and 10 percent criticism.

Are you a positive communicator with people? It will be far easier for them to reach out to you and share, if your orientation is positive.

The apostle Paul gave excellent guidance about the proper emphasis of our attitude and lifestyle when he wrote, "Finally brethren, whatever is true, whatever is honorable, whatever is right, whatever is pure, whatever is lovely, whatever is of good repute, if there is any excellence and if anything is worthy of praise, let your mind dwell on these things" (Philippians 4:8, NASB).

Be encouraging and let your conversation be positive. Compare the following statements and I'm sure you'll recognize which is most motivating.

"You never give me flowers anymore!"

"I have so appreciated the wonderful times you gave me flowers."

Dottie is a constant encourager. When I get down emotionally from my heavy schedule, when I become negative and discouraged, she will say, "You're tired, darling, but think of all the people you have helped." She accentuates the positive.

6. Practice Confidentiality

What a plus factor it is in communication when your mate knows that you are able to keep things to yourself. There's automatically a greater willingness to be open with you. If you are a gossip—one who habitually talks about other people—you raise an immediate barrier to others sharing intimately with you, for fear that you will make their innermost feelings public. In speaking I regularly use personal illustrations to amplify my points, but I must be very careful of what I share about my relationship with Dottie. If I were to speak too openly about the intimacies of our relationship, Dottie inevitably would have to become cautious and defensive.

A young lady named Joyce asked to talk to me about her situation with Wendel. Wendel wanted the relationship to develop along more serious lines toward marriage, and was pressing Joyce to define the extent of her commitment to him. Joyce wasn't quite sure of her feelings. In a long talk with Wendel she had shared how hesitant she was to make future commitments because of some personal areas she felt she first needed to work through.

Wendel, out of frustration, had gone to a number of people for counsel (and sympathy). In seeking their advice, he had shared what Joyce had confided in him. When it got back to Joyce, she became very defensive. She felt her privacy had been invaded and was understandably finding it difficult to be open with him.

Do you keep things to yourself? Or do you gossip and tell others "in confidence"? Publicly airing private matters destroys the trust in a marriage. When one spouse feels betrayed, it becomes much harder to be transparent the next time.

7. Wait for the Right Time

"Timely advice is as lovely as golden apples in a silver basket," we read in Proverbs 25:11. Proverbs 15:23 echoes, "How wonderful it is to be able to say the right thing at the right time!" In a relationship, dialogue will be enhanced if the right words are spoken *at the right time*. And love must be your guide as to when and where you share bad news or discuss a difficult subject.

My mother always said that if she had something difficult to tell my dad, she would feed him first. Telling him bad news when he was hungry was to her a major tactical error. She knew that if she told him after he had eaten, he could handle it better. In relationships with roommates, spouses, friends, or with anyone, we must be sensitive not only to the way we speak, but also to the timing involved. "Good news, bad news" jokes are funny really because they are based on this principle.

Often, depending upon the situation, it may be best to wait until morning to share something controversial with your spouse. This is especially true if he or she has had a very difficult day. Dottie explains her approach to timing this way, "I'm a very communicative person— it's important to me. And I've always wanted to have a relationship where we communicated about everything all of the time; which I still do. But I learned early in our marriage that if I had something to tell Josh that was very important—a problem, something I was struggling with, or any heavy subject at all—I needed to choose carefully not only how I told him, but when.

"There are times when he doesn't want something heavy; like ten minutes before he gets up to speak (or maybe even the day of a talk). If there's a real problem with one of the children or if I'm feeling hurt, I often don't tell him then. When somebody is about to face 700 people, you don't tell him things that can preoccupy his mind and diminish his effectiveness, no matter how serious they may be. I also try to avoid laying something heavy on Josh before he goes to sleep because it will disrupt his sleep. He's got a real active mind. So unless it's an absolute emergency, I'll wait until morning."

8. Share Your Feelings

A vulnerability that allows you to share feelings, inner thoughts, deep hurts and great joys is essential to a healthy climate of intimacy and closeness. Learn to say *how you feel* in conversation as well as *what you think*. Partners can argue over thoughts and ideas, but feelings cannot be debated. They can only be acknowledged. So coming to understand each other's emotions is the gateway to psychological intimacy. When there is no regular expression of feeling between a couple, they will remain locked out of the love and intimacy that is their treasure.

The Bloods, co-therapists and co-authors of *Marriage,* describe the couple who avoids confrontation: "By suppressing hostile feelings and avoiding overt conflicts, they often end up with escalated resentment, frustration, anger. Holding in your gripes can lay the groundwork for future violence, withdrawal, depression and even ill health (ulcers and asthma, for example). 'Suffering in silence,' warn the Bloods, 'erodes trust, intimacy and growth.'"[5]

"Marriage is intended to be an intimate relationship built upon mutual understanding between husband and wife," writes marriage and family psychologist, Dr. J. Allen Peterson. "For this communion of heart to occur, conversation must go beyond the level of home and children to include a sharing of thoughts and feelings in the experiences of daily living."[6] So often we talk only about the mundane—keeping our innermost feelings to ourselves. Yet the ability to share intimately is crucial to a fulfilled love and marriage relationship.

Lines of communication must be kept open especially on the feelings level. This means mutually agreeing "...to share negative feelings whenever they arise, without bitterness if possible. For instance, you could say, 'Honey, you've done something that makes me mad, and I don't want to be mad with you. If I tell you about it, will you help me to understand just why I feel so hostile?' This may not always work, but it often will. The principle is try not to swallow or bury any of your negative feelings (of which you will generate plenty) toward each other, but to bring them out into the light of understanding. If all married couples learned to do just that, they would put most marriage counselors out of business."[7]

Men will often regard sharing emotions and feelings as a sign of weakness. They think that crying and admitting to being wrong is not "macho." Men tend more toward intellectual and rational arguments than to feelings. Norman Wright explains the predicament in which men find themselves when they are "not comfortable sharing their failures, anxieties, disappointments. An indicator of being a man is 'I can do it by myself. I don't need any help.' Unfortunately this leads to the inability to say 'help me' when help is desperately needed."[8]

9. Avoid Mind-reading

Warning: Don't take it for granted that the other person understands your gestures, the tone of your voice or your body language. It becomes very frustrating in a relationship when each person assumes the other knows what he or she is thinking and feeling and wants to do. Mind-reading rarely works and never consistently. You can't hold your spouse responsible for responding to your hurts, needs, or feelings of joy or thanksgiving if you haven't verbalized them. Everyone has to speak up!

"I take full blame for a conflict with Josh on our honeymoon," Dottie admits. "We were in Mexico and driving to Acapulco, which put us in the car together for several hours. I was a new bride and thought, 'I'm married to this man, but he doesn't know everything there is to know about me. I even have some close girlfriends that know more about me than my own husband does! If we're going to be married, he should know everything about me.' (It didn't occur to me that we had a lifetime ahead of us to get acquainted). So, I thought I'd better tell him just how I felt about everything, so he could really know his wife.

"The time span between our first date and our marriage had been just over six months, so I knew there was a lot I hadn't been able to tell Josh in that short dating period. I was feeling the need to share, so I proceeded to talk and talk while Josh watched for road signs and fumbled with maps. I would tell him something and get no response. I would tell him something else, and get a 'Huh. Well, that's interesting.' And the more I shared, the less feedback I got—he was preoccupied with other things. I was getting angrier all the time, but I didn't know how to say, 'You are hurting my feelings because I don't feel like you are interested.' I just assumed that since I was talking, he should listen, so in my frustration I quit talking.

"As the clock ticked on in silence, I continued to grow angrier. The problem was, he was still off somewhere else and had absolutely no idea about what was going on in my mind. Josh has a wonderful ability to concentrate and think about several things at once while blocking out his surroundings. However, in those beginning days I really didn't understand that, and I expected him to be extremely absorbed in me when I talked.

"By the time we reached Acapulco I could hardly see straight. I got out of the car and told him I was furious. 'Why?' he asked. I said, 'Because you didn't even talk to me all the way down!' Poor Josh didn't have the foggiest idea that I had wanted to talk or why I was so mad, because at that point in our relationship I didn't know how to communicate my feelings.

"He was so totally baffled by the whole thing that he got perturbed at me, so we just fumed at each other for a while. He finally took the initiative in apologizing for not talking and admitted that he was insensitive and was really sorry. And that made me feel bad because I had flown off the handle like that.

"That was our first real misunderstanding, and it gave me a glimpse of how important it is to verbalize feelings and thoughts. You have to express your true feelings and deal with them, not stuff them down inside. Going back over that whole incident and rehearsing our feelings has helped us to understand each other better, and to turn it into a positive learning experience."

Dangerous Assumptions

When your friend or spouse does something that hurts your feelings, you have to let him or her know. Don't just assume or hope that he or she will figure it out and come to you first. Every relationship would become more harmonious and more intimate if we would just stop assuming and start communicating our feelings. When Dottie doesn't tell me something, I often don't get it because I do not read her body language (and still have trouble reading her mind). And when I am not willing to listen, she is usually not willing to share. When I do not make an effort to change, she is not motivated to change either.

Listen to how Leo Buscaglia describes the danger of burying our emotions: "If we hold them in long enough, especially negative emotions, we're bound to explode; they're bound to come out at a time where it's inappropriate. If we store it up, it's usually an innocent person who does some small thing and we blast them with all this stored up anger."[9]

Dottie relates that at various times early in our marriage she failed to express her frustration over my apparent insensitivity. She explains, "I can walk into a room and intuitively know if someone is hurting—I can see it in their eyes. Conversely, Josh seldom senses it on his own. But, if you tell him you've got a problem, he'll find a solution for you before he leaves. All I have to do is to tell him I'm hurting and his compassion takes over. Since I don't need to be told when someone needs a shoulder or a boost, it's easy for me to expect him to be able to read my feelings at a glance.

"One day I was feeling huffy because I thought he wasn't being sensitive to me. Here was Josh speaking at a free-speech forum, sharing the gospel with these people—cool, together, totally in control while antagonists threw insults and accusations at him. Here I was at the back of this huge crowd when it hit me—if he were as sensitive and in tune with what every individual was feeling as I tend to be, he could never do what he's doing now. He can't afford to get his feelings hurt every time someone lies about him or insults him. So in a sense God protected him by not making him overly sensitive. I am in tune with individuals, he is in tune with the crowd, and God just made it very clear to me how well we complement each other and are most effective—together.

"When you're first married, it takes a while to understand where the other person is coming from and how God has designed him or her. You have to learn that your unique traits are not better or worse than your mate's, just different. My problem was that I was rather afraid to tell Josh when he acted differently from what I expected. I wanted him to figure it out for himself. And being newly married, I thought it would take all of the magic out of it if he changed only when I pointed things out to him.

"For example: We decided at the very beginning that we would view possessions in terms of 'ours' which was not easy at first. I had a brand new little Maverick that I had bought, and which I assumed Josh would treat just as my father had. As I was growing up I adored and respected the way my father kept his cars immaculately clean—no fingerprints on the window, no trash on the floor, and a thorough washing every Saturday.

"Josh thought of cars simply as transportation. He's not a slob, but it didn't bother him to set an empty Coke can on the floor and it wasn't his custom to wash the car every Saturday.

"Several weeks after our honeymoon, I was baffled because he hadn't once suggested we wash the car. I had always assumed that men who were responsible did that. I figured it was part of the husband's role, and I didn't adjust to Josh's style at first. I kept thinking, 'My dad doesn't let his car get this dirty,' and I would make comments about how my dad always kept the car nice, and how my dad did this and that. Josh wasn't comparing me to his mother or to anyone else, but I was comparing him to my dad.

"The man who loved me most before Josh kept a spotless car, and I was feeling that if a man didn't keep his car clean, he must be communicating something other than love. I held these feelings in and let them fester until they came to a boil. When I finally told Josh how he was keeping our car and what I was feeling, he immediately became more sensitive to me and how I felt. I realized I should have shared my feelings long before. And I also realized the obvious: that you don't have to keep your car spotless and sanitized to be a good person!

"When people get married, they usually have talked through the big things, like finances, number of children, and so on, so those are pretty much out of the way. It's the little things you would never think about that you have to talk about and work through. And part of the great joy in becoming one is in working these things out together."

Not a single couple has ever simply awakened one morning magically able to share their deepest feelings. It's a learning process. It takes time for you and your spouse to become comfortable with reaching down and sharing those sensitive parts. And one of the greatest challenges of love is to get to know each other's threshold for expressing feelings.

10. Give a Response to Show You're Listening.

If there is one thing that always encourages sharing, it is giving either verbal or body language feedback. As one woman, hurt and frustrated from a total lack of response, was heard to exclaim, "If you're listening to me, respond! Say something. Say anything. Just let me know that you're listening to me!" When our heart reaches out to others, it yearns for acknowledgment.

Here are some helpful suggestions to show that you are absorbing what another is saying:

React physically. Turn toward the person. Lean forward. Nod your head in response. Keep looking the person in the eyes. Nothing shows greater interest than eye contact.

Request more information. Ask a question which seeks clarification or additional details: "What did you mean by that?" Or, "Why is that important to you?" In asking questions you are saying, "Tell me more— I'm interested."

Reflect on what has been said with a leading statement: "You seem quite excited by meeting him." Or, "That must have been rough on you." Reflective listening pays off in more intimate sharing.

Repeat or rephrase statements with feeling. Echoing the meaning or feeling of a statement both clarifies and encourages further communication.

Remain silent when someone is telling a story. Don't interrupt, and don't finish sentences for people. This is a hard one for me. I have to keep telling myself, "Don't interrupt, don't interrupt." Also, don't rush to fill a pause in the conversation simply to avoid the silence—you may cut off something important the person was preparing to share.

Dottie admits that "sometimes it makes me a little bit angry when Josh chimes in on my story. I feel like, 'Doesn't he think I can tell the story myself, or does he think I'm going into too much detail, or what?' Other times I realize that it's merely a reflection of his enthusiasm. He gets excited about what I'm going to tell him and he just jumps in—he doesn't see it as an intrusion or an interruption, or that he is taking anything away from me. I know he wants to join me in what I'm saying, but the best thing for me in sharing my feelings is when Josh lets me tell the story." Patience is a blessing.

Refrain from concentrating on your answer or rebuttal while another is still talking—it makes you impatient to speak. When you are constantly constructing a rebuttal or a way to justify something you've said, you are merely building up a defense mechanism. As a result you are not truly listening.

Margaret Lane in her book *Are You Really Listening?* shares an embarrassing moment that resulted from not listening actively: "Years ago, fresh out of college and being interviewed for a job on a small-town newspaper, I learned the hard way. My interview had been going well, and the editor, in an expansive mood, began telling me about his winter ski trip. Eager to make a big impression with a tale of my own about backpacking in the same mountains, I tuned him out and started planning *my* story. 'Well,' he asked suddenly, 'What do you think of that?' Not having heard a word, I babbled foolishly, 'Sounds like a marvelous holiday—great fun!' For a moment he stared at me. 'Fun?' he asked in an icy tone. 'How could it be fun? I've just told you I spent most of it hospitalized with a broken leg.'"[10]

Express your encouragement and appreciation for what the other person has been sharing. Both of these enhance healthy communication. Solomon, in all his wisdom, knew that "kind words are like honey—enjoyable and healthful" (Proverbs, 15:24). Say, "Thanks so much for sharing that. I'm sure it wasn't easy, but I really appreciate it." Or, "What you've said makes a lot of sense, and I know it's going to help."

These techniques are just a few of the best ways to actively be a better listener. Remember that your ear can open the door to another's heart, so don't close it. Believe me, if you work on being a better listener, it will pay off. Just ask Dottie! She has seen me change.

11. Be Honest.

The apostle Paul saw the issue clearly when he admonished us to "speak the truth in love" (Ephesians 4:15). To speak the truth in love means to take into consideration the other person's feelings. A truly skillful and loving communicator is sensitive to the consequences of his words and actions.

Solomon gave wise counsel when he said, "Do you see a man who is hasty in his words? There is more hope for a fool than for him" (Proverbs. 29:20). "Love," writes Richard Strauss, "will help us preface our remarks with some word of commendation or appreciation, and we will present our thoughts pleasantly, constructively, and positively. We will encourage rather than injure our mates."[11]

The barriers to being honest are numerous. One is simply that it's risky. "All deep relationships," according to Dr. H. Norman Wright, "especially marriage relationships, must be based on absolute openness and honesty. This may be difficult to achieve because it involves a risk—the risk of being rejected because of our honesty, but it is vital for relationships to grow in marriage."[12]

When we feel we need to be honest in something that could hurt another, we not only need to review the style in which we deliver the message, but we also need to examine our motives. Many very cruel things have been said in the name of "honesty."

Another barrier is that honesty can become nit-picky. Honesty can open a person up, only to reveal that a complete record is on file of every personal flaw. Honest communication, spoken in love and heard in love, does not "keep score." As a result, when "loving communication" takes place you can share what is most genuine—imperfections and all.

Speaking the truth in love also involves verbalizing your love for another in *words*:

"Thank you for just being you."

"I'm proud of you."

"Thanks for loving me."

"I'm so glad I'm married to you."

"I love just being with you."

Also speaking the truth in love requires care not to exaggerate or disguise. Dr. Wright tells the story of a woman "who acquired wealth and decided to have a book written about her genealogy. The well-known author she engaged for the assignment discovered that one of her grandfathers had been electrocuted in Sing Sing. When he said it would have to be included in the book, she pleaded for a way of saying it that would hide the truth.

"When the book appeared, it read as follows: 'One of her grandfathers occupied the chair of applied electricity in one of America's best-known institutions. He was very much attached to his position and literally died in the harness.'" Wright emphasizes that "the meaning in some attempts to communicate between marriage partners gets almost as obscure and confusing. It is usually better to 'say it like it is,' gently if necessary, but clearly."[13]

Being an effective, skillful communicator is a major tool in becoming the "right person," and you can start right where you are. If you are single, begin to practice these principles with your friends and on dates. If you are married, begin with your spouse. With your example, and loving, honest patience, encourage your mate to grow with you as a communicator.

As in acquiring a foreign language, learning to communicate skillfully takes time, dedication, focus and practice. Some of us may be better at it than others, so patience with them and ourselves is necessary. But every one of us can continue to improve.

To get started, select one life situation where more effective communication can make a big difference. Now plan an approach using several of the principles. Set a time when you will implement the plan.

Questions to Ponder

- What are the two main aspects of communication?
- What are key elements of good communication?
- Why is listening an important aspect of communication?
- What are the different levels of listening?

FURTHER HELPFUL RESOURCES:
Dr. David Augsburger, *Caring Enough To Hear And Be Heard*, (Ventura, CA: Regal Books, 1982).
Roger and Donna Vann, *Secrets of a Growing Marriage* (San Bernardino, CA; Here's Life Publishers, 1985).
H. Norman Wright, *The Family That Listens*, (Wheaton, IL: Victor Books, 1981).
Richard B. Wilke, *Tell Me Again, I'm Listening*, (Nashville, TN: Abingdon Press, 1977).
H. Norman Wright, *Communication: Key To Your Marriage*, (Ventura, CA: Regal Books, 1983).
H. Norman Wright, *More Communication Keys For Your Marriage*, (Ventura, CA: Regal Books, 1983).

6

RESOLVING CONFLICT

How can you be true to the kind of person God made you to be and still be at peace with others? Not many of us succeed, especially in that most intimate of relationships, marriage.

"I've got to get in touch with myself," a seventeen-year veteran of marriage experience confessed. "My value system has always been radically different from my wife's, even after we became Christians. To avoid conflict I suppressed my feelings, my desires and beliefs. I cannot do that any longer, even though I consider myself a servant."

A wife of fourteen years confessed, "I expected my husband to give me the same love and affection I had experienced in my first marriage. When I did not get it I unconsciously sought to gain it by avoiding all conflict. Only after we were divorced did I discover he considered me gutless because I consistently avoided conflict."

Such behavior is not limited to marriage. In society, in business, and in the church we often act as though conflict is abnormal. That it is not was recognized by no less an authority than the apostle Paul, who suggests a key reason for conflict in Romans 12:4,5: "For just as we have many members in one body and all the members do not have the same function, so we, who are many, are one body in Christ, and individually members of one another."

The very fact that we are different makes conflict inevitable. We bring different backgrounds, viewpoints, emotions, and even different cultures into our relationships. Whenever two living people come together there will be conflict sooner or later. *Having conflict*, then, is not the issue. The real test is whether you and I can *resolve conflict*.

Unfortunately, many of us carry the reactions to conflict we learned before we became Christians into our new life. Somehow we don't recognize that Jesus modeled an entirely different response to conflict.

Believers who have appropriated the Holy Spirit's power, can learn to meet conflict head-on and genuinely resolve it in truth and love.

When this does not happen, our witness for Jesus Christ is clouded. You may recall Eldridge Cleaver, one of the black activist leaders who orchestrated a lot of rebellion and violence against the police and establishment in the late '60s and early '70s. News reports several years ago revealed he had become a Christian. Yet later he turned from evangelical Christianity to become a Mormon. In an interview he said, "I could not understand and grasp the conflict that goes on between Christians."

Working Against Ourselves

Our serious inability to cope with conflicts is exhibited daily in the workplace. I am amazed at how quickly people seek a job change after running into a conflict at work. Most would rather go through the effort of finding and taking a different position than attempting to resolve the tension in their current relationship. It's simply a preference of flight over fight.

When I was in Israel I had the privilege of visiting one of the ancient fortresses in Caesarea. There I was reminded that people throughout history have been trying to protect themselves against vulnerability. This Caesarean fort had a so-called "dry moat"—a broad open space around it containing no water. Anyone who crossed the moat was completely exposed. The castle main gate was similarly designed. It was located sideways to the entrance, thereby exposing the vulnerable parts of the body and armor of anyone who turned to enter it.

As I walked about that fortress I thought about the millions of people who go through life constantly trying to insulate themselves against being vulnerable and hurt. They crave and search for real emotional intimacy, but they can never find it in their relationships because they are emotionally unable to resolve the conflicts which always arise in long-term, intimate relationships. This is why there are so few lasting relationships today.

Overcoming Two Fears

Earlier I mentioned two fears haunting people today: the fear that they will never be loved and the fear they will never be able to love. As Christians these same fears enter into our relationship with God. We harbor an inner fear that God cannot love us and that He will not consider our love acceptable to Him. God uses other people to give His love real arms so we can believe and experience it. You and I often need another person to make God's love real to us.

Yet, as the intimacy in relationships God intended for you and me grows, so does the potential for conflict. The intricacies of two individuals growing in their knowledge of each other provides a much greater potential for conflict than even the relationship between two super-powers. Working through the inter-personal maze can be more involved than two warring nations conducting peace talks. Thus, not surprisingly, people who develop real intimacy may also begin to back off a bit, for with deeper intimacy comes potential for greater conflict. They may never have learned how to cope with this facet of intimacy.

To Resolve or Dissolve

There is a phrase I want you to remember. It is simply this: *It is more rewarding to resolve a conflict than to dissolve a relationship.* Of course, it is much easier just to walk away than to put forth the effort to resolve a conflict. But the reward of staying is that every time you resolve a conflict you come out a better person—better able to deal with the inevitable conflicts the future will bring.

Sometimes we forget that relationships are part of God's initial grand design. God said in Genesis 2:18, "It is not good for man to be alone. I will make a helper suitable for him." I believe that God is speaking here beyond the marital relationship. You and I were created not to be alone, but to have relationships. But to experience the blessing that God intended for us to have in relationships we must go against the false wisdom of our day and resolve our conflicts.

Today you are encouraged to demand your rights and "have it your way." The Army seeks recruits using the slogan: "Be all that you can be"; and another advertising slogan reminds you that "you deserve a break today." Our culture's emphasis is clearly on you, the individual, and not your relationships. The elevation of self above others has created an "I'm number 1" philosophy which does not teach us to build lasting relationships and to resolve conflict. If winning is everything for you, you may reach a few personal goals, but you will sacrifice relationships along the way. Relationships are built by yielding, not winning. We must therefore rise above our culture if we want to experience intimate, fulfilled relationships. I believe that, through Christ, you and I can do that.

Turning Negatives to Positives

Have you ever felt good after resolving a conflict? If so, you will agree that there are positive benefits from conflict. I know that I have become a sharper, more useful instrument in the hands of the Holy Spirit because of how God has used conflicts with people in my life. Proverbs 27:17 instructs that "as iron sharpens iron, so one man sharpens another." I have become more sensitive to the hurts and feelings of other people as a result of conflict. Romans 5:3,4 explains that tribulation brings about perseverance and proven character. God uses conflict in my life to develop these inner qualities.

Ineffective Responses

Conversely, we often make a variety of negative responses to conflict. By examining several of these I think we can each better recognize how to handle conflict and its effects on our relationships.

Failing to acknowledge the problem or the conflict is the first negative response. I call it the "everything is great" syndrome. The person or subject of the conflict is ignored and the conflict simply goes unresolved.

Withdrawal is another response. You give conflict "the silent treatment." You don't talk about it and hide by staying away from the person or source of the conflict. Interestingly enough, this was the response of Adam and Eve to God in the Garden of Eden. The Bible says, "They hid themselves." They withdrew and God had to go looking for them. I have found that the more I talk to a person who has chosen "the silent treatment," the more silent that person becomes. And raising my voice to evoke some type of response often backfires and turns the confrontation toward more violent expressions.

Ignoring the conflict's significance is a third response. "It doesn't matter" becomes our slogan. In this situation the offended person imagines, "It doesn't matter because he or she won't listen to me anyway," or "It doesn't matter because he or she won't change," or even, "It'll blow over." Dealing with the conflict superficially and flippantly doesn't remove it. Instead it gives it an ideal chance to grow into a much larger eruption.

Spiritualizing is a fourth unhealthy way of dealing with conflict. The often heard comment, "Well, praise the Lord!" is quickly followed by a reciting of Romans 8:28, "All things work together for good." But too often the truth really is that sincerity is lacking and that this approach is merely another avoidance tactic.

Keeping score is a fifth response. Conflicts and feelings of anger and resentment become bottled up inside. An explosion is inevitable. Philippians 3:13 exhorts us instead to use the spiritual fire extinguisher of "forgetting the past." I think all marriage partners should have a policy that nothing can be brought up in an argument that happened more than three months earlier. One man went to see a marriage counselor and complained, "Every time I get into a fight with my wife, she gets historical!"

The counselor interrupted, "Don't you mean hysterical?"

"No, I mean, historical!" the man replied. "She always brings up the past!" That's scorekeeping.

Attacking the person instead of the problem is a sixth often used negative response. I saw an example of this recently when a person involved in a borderline group of evangelical Christianity asked me, "Did you read what so-and-so wrote about such-and-such?" I said I had. Then she immediately proceeded to attack the writer—not what he had written. "Do you know he's been divorced three times?" she complained. Instead of dealing with the issue and resolving the conflict, she attacked the person.

Blaming someone else is a seventh way people deal with conflicts. This usually indicates an inability on the part of the the person doing the blaming to acknowledge his or her own failures. Adam and Eve's reaction (Genesis 3:9-13) after they ate the forbidden fruit is a perfect example. God asked, "What did you do?"

Adam answered, "The woman You gave me, she gave me the fruit." First Adam blamed God and then the woman.

Eve's response was, "The serpent deceived me." Both were blaming someone else.

Desiring to win no matter what the cost and *giving in just to avoid the conflict* are two more negative responses. Neither of these postures resolves anything. In both cases only one of the parties goes away with the feeling that something was accomplished. Furthermore both of these tactics always create resentment.

Buying a special gift for the other person is a tenth poor response to conflict. This is an especially favorite ploy of husbands. Instead of dealing with the conflict, these people try to buy their way out of it.

Solutions Start Here

You may have recognized yourself in one or even several of these negative ways of dealing with conflict. If so, you will be glad to know that there are positive and constructive ways of dealing with conflict. Each starts with your commitment to the lordship of Jesus Christ. Spiritual maturity is evidenced not by a lack of conflict, but by dealing with it biblically and without losing self-control. Your desire to resolve conflict will also depend upon your commitment to the relationship. The closer you are to the other person, the more willing you will be to work through a conflict.

When I got married, I said, "I do," and I meant it. Come hell or high water, I am committed to working out every conflict Dottie and I will encounter.

When our son, Sean, was just six years old, he asked me one day, "Daddy, are you going to leave Mommy?" I asked why he wanted to know. He told me that several of his friends' fathers were divorcing their wives.

I realized that children even from secure homes are beginning to have the same fears as children from broken homes.

So I looked Sean right in the eye, raised my voice a little and said, "Son, I love your mother. I am committed to your mother, and I will never leave her, period!" He gave a sigh of relief and said, "Thanks, Dad!" He wasn't looking for a reinforcement of my commitment to him. He needed to know that I was committed to his mother, because the permanence of our marriage relationship is really where his security comes from.

Truths to Live By

I want to share with you some principles I try to live by each day. I don't always accomplish them, but it is my heart's desire to apply these truths to my life daily, especially in the area of inter-personal conflicts. Perhaps they will help you.

The first principle deals with personal attitudes: *Acknowledge that you are fallible.* Accepting criticism and admitting to your mistakes is one of the first attitudes to develop in resolving conflict. The Bible offers good advice in Proverbs 13:18: "If you refuse criticism, you will end in poverty and disgrace; if you accept criticism you are on the road to fame" (TLB). So, when you are wrong, admit it. When you are right, don't say anything. That is a sound policy for resolving a conflict.

Paul assures us in Philippians 1:6, "For I am confident of this very thing, that He who began a good work in you will perfect it until the day of Christ Jesus." No mistake you can make is fatal. God is greater than your greatest goofs. And through constructive criticism He is able to use our mistakes to make us better individuals and better lovers of Him and other people. That is why we read in Proverbs 28:13, "A man who refuses to admit his mistakes can never be successful. But if he confesses and forsakes them, he gets another chance" (TLB).

Paul wrote in Romans 14:13, "Let us therefore stop turning critical eyes on one another. If we must be critical, let us be critical of our own conduct and see that we do nothing to make a brother stumble or fall" (Phillips). In dealing with conflict, the attitude I seek to express is, "Lord, I want You to resolve this conflict, and please start with me."

A second principle I follow is to *take responsibility for my emotional reactions.* We cannot blame another person for our temper and outbursts of anger. Anger should be our reaction to an unjust situation, not to the faults of another individual. In his book, *Caring Enough to Hear And Be Heard,* David Augsburger puts it this way: "When a fault in you provokes anger in me, then I know that your fault is my fault, too. If I have made peace with the same area within myself, my anger will not be aroused by the sight of it in you. But when I hear you saying the very thing I hate to hear from myself, I feel inner turmoil."[1] When people get angry with someone else it is often because they see in that person a negative quality that they also see in themselves.

Next, I want to stress the importance of *seeing the other person's side* in a conflict. The apostle Paul writes in Romans 10:2, "For I bear them witness that they have a zeal for God, but not in accordance with knowledge." He explained that he knew exactly where they were coming from. He had been there, and could identify with them. This posture is called empathy.

You are probably familiar with the sound counsel in the old Indian proverb, "Do not criticize a man until you have walked a mile in his moccasins." Try to experience the conflict from the other person's point of view. And then try to recognize that an intellectual understanding of it is one thing, but to really feel it in your emotions is quite another. You will find out that the other person in the conflict will have a valid basis for his or her feelings. In order to resolve the conflict, you have to genuinely try to see the problem as the other person sees it.

This kind of empathy is often very difficult. But as Paul in Philippians 2:3,4 reminds us, "Never act from motives of rivalry or personal vanity, but in humility think more of each other than you do of yourselves. None of you should think only of his own affairs, but should learn to see things from other people's points of view" (Phillips New Testament). In other words, we need to look beyond our hurt to see the other person's hurt. To do this you will have to ask God to help you.

One technique that has helped me is forcing myself to be as resourceful in understanding the other person as I am in trying to get him to understand me. St. Francis of Assisi said, "Lord, grant that I may seek more to understand than to be understood." Can you imagine what would happen in our relationships if we all held this attitude? Most conflicts would quickly dissolve, because most are the result of each person holding to a different assumption.

If you want to handle your conflicts in a biblical way you must remember this question: What does God want to teach me in this conflict? Whatever it is, I can learn from it.

A Winning Formula

Let me show you a fabulous four-point outline for resolving conflict found in the first five verses of chapter 7 in the Gospel according to Matthew. Verses 1 and 2 say, "Do not judge lest you be judged. For in the way you judge you will be judged; and by your standard or measurement, it will be measured to you." This tells us to *be humble*. Verse 3 follows, "And why do you look at the speck that is in your brother's eye, but do not notice the log that is in your own eye?" Here we are clearly told to *be honest*. I don't think I have ever been involved in a conflict where there wasn't a log in my own eye.

Then, in verse 4 we read, "Or how can you say to your brother, 'Let me take the speck out of your eye,' and behold the log in your own eye?" The lesson here is *integrity*. And finally, in verse 5 we are commanded to deal with conflict *in love*: "You hypocrite, first take the log out of your own eye, and then you will see clearly to take the speck out of your brother's eye." Jesus has called us to be humble, to be honest, to exercise integrity and to demonstrate love.

Here's the danger. You can get wrapped up so easily in seeking revenge and in wanting to get even in a conflict that you miss what God wants you to learn in the situation. The focus should be on finding out what God is saying to *you*. This requires a willingness to admit that you are not perfect. Your prayer and mine ought to be, "Lord, give me the strength to admit my shortcomings." Admitting is not a sign of weakness. Rather it takes courage to admit that you are wrong. As you acknowledge a weakness in your own life, you immediately become more able to accept a weakness in someone else's life.

A willingness to be corrected is another requirement if you are to learn God's lesson for you. We can easily be more blind to our own faults than someone else's.

A proper attitude and willingness to change are also vital. In every situation you should have the desire to come out a better person, a better servant and a better friend. With these attitudes you will set the Holy Spirit free to do His work.

Remember, especially when dealing with conflict, that love covers many sins. The apostle Peter reminds us, "Above all, keep fervent in your love for one another, because love covers a multitude of sins," (1 Peter 4:8). I see so many Christians who feel they have to be the conscience for the body of Christ. Somehow they think it is spiritual to point out every fault and mistake they see. Paul sets the pattern in Romans 15:1, "Now we who are strong [or mature] ought to bear the weaknesses of those without strength and not just please ourselves." So often we try to do the work of the Holy Spirit.

If you truly love a person, you will bear that person's weakness and take it upon yourself. I have met some people whose faith would have been destroyed if I had gone to see a movie. They simply do not believe it is right to go to a movie theater. In that type of a situation I do not quickly point out their weakness and insist on my right to see a movie. Instead, I spend time with the individual, and it is amazing to see how God will bring the person to say, "I can see your point."

Love covers a multitude of sins and bears the weaknesses. In Ephesians 4:2 Paul calls it "making allowances for each other's faults because of your love" (TLB). You must be willing to compromise for the good of the other person. Note that this does not apply to moral issues, but to individual idiosyncrasies. In these areas of relationships, love is grace in action.

Active Solutions

Along with developing some of these attitudes I have just discussed, there are specific actions you can take which will aid you in resolving conflict.

Begin by *seeking knowledge* in two areas.

First, *search the Scriptures* about the area of conflict which you are experiencing. I have often been able to find situations similar to the one I am going through in the Bible.

Second, *search for facts* about the other person and the situation. I agree with Proverbs 18:13: "He who gives an answer before he hears, it is folly and shame to him." Many conflicts arise from misunderstandings and false assumptions about something that was said.

Some time back, Dottie was having tea with a close friend who made a comment about one of our children. Dottie perceived it as very negative. She was so stunned and hurt that she excused herself and went to the bedroom. Later that week Dottie happened to be preparing a talk on confrontation. As she worked on it she realized that she needed to put her convictions into action, and to talk to this young woman. This was not easy, for Dottie does not like relationships to be uncomfortable. But the friendship could not continue until the matter was cleared up. As they talked, Dottie realized that she had perceived incorrectly what her friend had said, and the problem was resolved very quickly simply by determining the facts.

Prayer is another way to take action. Pray first for wisdom. James promises us, "But if any of you lacks wisdom, let him ask of God, who gives to all men generously and without reproach, and it will be given to him" (James 1:5). Now don't mistake wisdom for knowledge. Wisdom aids us in properly using knowledge.

Pray specifically for the other person by name. God will change your attitude toward the individual and enable you to deal better with the problem. "Pray for one another," is good advice from James.

Prayer must be made in faith. In James 1:6 we read, "But let him ask in faith without any doubting." Often my prayer goes something like this, "Father, from a human perspective, I don't know how this conflict could ever be resolved, but I know it's not honoring to You to dissolve the relationship. So, by faith, I am trusting You to use me, Your word and other people to resolve this conflict."

Pray, finally, for the person's success. Peter reminds us, "Not returning evil for evil, or insult for insult, but giving a blessing instead" (1 Peter 3:9).

Seek wise counsel is the third action point. We are reminded in Proverbs 12:15, "The way of a fool is right in his own eyes. But a wise man is he who listens to counsel." As you seek counsel, however, be cautious. Our emotions usually run high when we are involved in a conflict situation and tend to blind us to our own faults and contribution to the conflict.

This warning comes from my personal experience. Unfortunately, I have a tendency to seek counsel from those who I know will agree with me and reinforce my positions. So I have to remind myself that I am seeking counsel not to win, but to resolve a conflict.

Dealing with your emotions first is another important step to take.

Ephesians 4:26 gives us the guideline, "Do not let the sun go down on your wrath." This verse does not forbid anger, but rather it admonishes us to deal with it promptly. If you don't control your anger, it will control you. Those feelings of anger and hurt which have not been resolved will stir your imagination, and as time goes by the facts will become more and more distorted, and bitterness will set in. If you don't deal with your emotions immediately, Satan will have a field day with you.

Keep a Clean Slate

I recently became quite concerned about the number of evangelical Christians in visible positions who have fallen into sexual immorality and divorce. I shared my concern with a close friend and with Dottie. As we talked specifically about what we had been doing to keep our relationship healthy, she brought up an interesting point. She mentioned that in all our years of marriage, I had never once left home without resolving a conflict we may have had.

There was the time I reached the car, turned around and went back to the house to apologize, and the time I drove three blocks in a snow storm, only to turn around and drive back home. Then Dottie made a statement which I think is very significant. She said, "You can leave for three months, and if there is nothing wrong in our relationship, I can handle it. But if you were ever to leave with something unresolved in our relationship, I couldn't handle it. Bitterness and resentment would set in, and it would become like a pebble in my shoe."

I don't think it is healthy even to leave for work in the morning without resolving a conflict. My wife and I practice this faithfully. Similarly, we try never to go to sleep if there is anything that needs to be resolved.

Recently I learned something about my wife I didn't know. My hair is thinning out a little so I had been using hair spray on it. We were both standing at the sink one morning when I picked up the hair spray and started using it. Dottie said to me, "Honey, please don't do that." Now, in fourteen years of marriage we had never discussed hair spray and I didn't know she not only hated it, but did not allow anyone to use it in the house.

So, thinking I would be very gracious, I stepped back from the sink and proceeded to use the spray. She said, "I told you it bothers me." Having already responded by stepping away, I got angry, threw down the hair spray which broke a bottle of her expensive cologne, and stormed out of the house.

As I drove toward a restaurant to have breakfast, I realized how insensitive I had been and asked God's forgiveness. Then as soon as I arrived, I headed for the phone and called home. When the phone rang at the house, Dottie told our son, "Sean, please pick up the phone.

It's your Dad." We talked through the incident and forgave each other for the way we had acted.

I think you can see by now that although you need to deal with your emotions immediately and before tackling the conflict, often they need to be given a little time. It can take a while before your feelings of hurt or anger dissipate and you are able to deal with the conflict without letting strong emotions interfere.

One day I received a strong letter from the pastor of a church in Colorado which had asked me to come and speak, canceling my engagement. He had talked to the deacons and elders of the church and they had decided I was charging too much money. So they asked me not to come. It was about four weeks later before I wrote back to them. I needed that time for my hurt to heal and for me to recover, as well as to give the church a chance to calm down. The letter I wrote was forty pages long, and I sent eight copies by Federal Express for the deacons.

Soon after that, I went to see the pastor, and the first thing he said to me was, "Can you ever forgive me?" Then he shared that the entire mission board had broken down crying when they read the letter, because they realized how badly they had treated many people over all the years of their existence. If I had written back to them in the heat of my emotions, we would have missed out on the joyous healing and a glorification of the body of Christ that resulted.

Remember the proverb, "How wonderful it is to be able to say the right thing at the right time" (Proverbs 15:23 TLB). I agree with verse 28: "A good man thinks before he speaks; the evil man pours out his evil words without a thought." My doctor says the reason I don't have an ulcer is probably because I laugh a lot, and because I tell people what I think. I do both, but in speaking my mind I always try to wait for the right time, for a calm emotional state and for the right motivation.

Checking Your Negatives

It is very important always to accentuate the good when involved in a conflict situation. Don't dwell on the negative, but rather on the positive aspects. Philippians 4:8 instructs, "For the rest, brethren, whatever is true, whatever is worthy of reverence and is honorable and seemly, whatever is just, whatever is pure, whatever is lovely and lovable, whatever is kind and winsome and gracious, if there is any virtue and excellence, if there is anything worthy of praise, think on and weigh and take account of these things — fix your mind on them."

Carefully ask yourself these questions:
1. Do you spend more time criticizing people in your mind than looking at their good points?
2. Do you talk about others in a derogatory manner behind their back?

3. Do you have a standard for others that you can't live up to yourself?
4. Do you pressure others to conform to your standards so that you can accept them more easily?

How you answer these questions says a lot about how you handle conflict.

There are people in my life who accept me just the way I am. Although they encourage me to become a better person, I know they will not love me any less if I never do. They dwell on the positives, not the negatives. Maybe you need to make more of an effort to accentuate the good, especially in your conflict situations.

Make sure the Holy Spirit is in control of your life is my last, but the most important, admonition. If you are not empowered by the Holy Spirit, you will find it difficult, if not impossible, to put these principles into action. He is the source who will enable you consistently to apply what you have learned and to lead you forward to the new insights still to be understood.

Questions to Ponder

- Why is it important to resolve conflict rather than walk away from a relationship?
- What are some negative responses to conflict?
- What are some attitudes to develop to help you deal with conflict?
- What are some actions you can take to resolve conflict?

FURTHER HELPFUL RESOURCES:
H. Norman Wright, *The Pillars Of Marriage* (Ventura, CA: Regal Books, 1980).
John Maxwell, *Your Attitude: Key to Success* (Here's Life Publishers).
Earl Wilson, *Loving Enough to Care* (Multnomah Press).
Josh McDowell, *Evidence For Joy* (Word Books).

7

LEARN TO FORGIVE

In Hawaii recently a very sharp looking gentleman and his wife sat down near me. We struck up a conversation and I inquired about his work. He explained that he was a consultant to corporations in the areas of personnel development and problems. When I asked what problem he encountered most he immediately replied, "Conflict."

So I asked, "What is the number one way you have found to resolve conflict?" Without batting an eye he responded, "Forgiveness." The greatest difficulty he faces is in challenging people to give up their bitterness and to give and accept forgiveness. This man, who wasn't a Christian, clearly understood the reconciling power of forgiveness.

When Billy Graham conducted his crusade in Honolulu, a group of twenty respected psychologists were sent to listen to his sermons and write up their criticism for the newspapers. They all agreed on one thing in their reports. When Dr. Graham called on people to repent and receive God's forgiveness his admonitions were psychologically sound.

You and I need to be forgiven. The director of a mental institution in Knoxville, Tennessee, said that 50 percent of the patients could go home if they only knew and believed they were forgiven.

We are living in a culture overrun with stored-up grudges, resentment, bitterness and broken hearts. Left unconfronted and unresolved these same problems affect the unity of the body of Christ, tear apart relationships, dull the cutting edge of the Holy Spirit in the lives of individuals, and divide everything from families to university movements. We need forgiveness!

The Oil of Relationships

Forgiveness is the oil of relationships. It reduces the friction and allows people to come close to one another. If you do not believe another individual is a forgiving person, you can never be truly open and vulnerable to him or her.

An unforgiving person is incapable of developing deep, lasting and intimate relationships. No matter how intelligent or skilled you may be; if you are an unforgiving person, you cannot develop an intimate relationship—it will be torn apart by unforgotten conflicts because they remain unforgiven.

Further, if you are unforgiving, loneliness is inevitable for you, because people will hesitate to be vulnerable around you. You will have built a barrier around yourself. Friendships without forgiveness don't last. For friendships to grow and become more intimate, there must be the security of knowing you can blow it again and again in the eyes of your friend and still be loved and totally forgiven.

An unforgiving partner in a marriage destroys the possibility of fulfilling the potential for intimacy in that relationship, especially in the area of communication. The other spouse will live in constant fear of offending, and thus be unwilling to communicate honestly for fear that the unforgiving mate will take advantage of his or her vulnerability. Bitterness and resentment will ultimately dominate that relationship.

Forgiveness when regularly practiced in marriage, however, leads to increased intimacy because it spawns open communication. If someone loves you despite your faults and accepts you even after you've wronged them, you can't help but respond to that person with an even deeper love.

Forgiveness is Like a Lens

Your views and practices regarding forgiveness largely determine how you deal with conflict. Ask yourself:

1. Do I see in each situation requiring forgiveness an opportunity to strengthen the relationship and to develop my own character?
2. Do I look to the needs of the one who has hurt me and try to understand him or her?
3. Do I realize that God will deal fairly with my offender if punishment is needed—that vengeance and retribution are not my responsibility?
4. Do I choose to thank God for each experience and allow His love and grace to grow in me as a result?

Relationships and marriages rarely break up over one single disagreement. Any explosion that erupts is usually only the latest in an accumulation of unforgiven and unreconciled conflicts.

Dr. Tim LaHaye writes, "Who of us is not subject to bad moods, ill temper, a negative spirit and a critical attitude? Admittedly these things should not exist in a Christian marriage, but they do. There is no married couple who, in the daily life of marriage, does not have a host of 'complaints.' Yet we see many such couples enjoying love, harmony, and peace in their relationship. Invariably, their secret is forgiveness."[1]

Let's face it, the Bible doesn't mince words when it comes to forgiveness. We are *commanded* to forgive. In Mark 11:25 Jesus tells us that when we are praying we are to forgive anything we have against anyone. Right after the Lord's prayer in Matthew 6 He says, "For if you forgive men for their transgressions, your heavenly Father will also forgive you. But if you do not forgive men, then your Father will not forgive your transgressions."

On first reading this would seem to say that our own forgiveness is based on our forgiveness of others, instead of on God's grace in Christ. However, that would contradict the rest of Christ's teachings. Instead, I believe Jesus is saying that if we refuse to forgive the person who has wronged us, God will thereby know that any confession of our own sins to Him must be less than genuine—that we have not really received the forgiveness which He has freely made available to us.

Richard Strauss writes, "A person who has honestly admitted to the vileness of his own sin and has experienced the blessing of God's forgiveness, cannot help but respond with forgiveness toward others."[2] And just as God's lovingkindness led us to repentance, isn't it possible that our lovingkindness to others, expressed through forgiveness, might help lead them to repentance?

Our standard for forgiving is Christ's—absolute and immediate. Yet most of us would never dream of forgiving some of the people He did. In Luke 7, we read about Christ forgiving the sinful woman; in John 8 he records Jesus forgiving the woman caught in adultery; He even forgave the men who crucified Him! In situations where we would have denounced others quickly or put them to shame, the constant description of the life of Christ is one of forgiveness.

What Is Forgiveness

How should forgiveness be defined? I have come across several definitions. I'm sure at least one of them will speak to you personally.

1. *Forgiveness* means: "To erase, to forego what is due;" "to give up resentment;" "to wipe the slate clean, to release from a debt, to cancel punishment;" "to personally accept the price of reconciliation;" "to give up all claims on one who has hurt you and let go the emotional consequences of that hurt." It not only means to say, "I forgive you," but it also means to give up the emotional consequences of the hurt. It means that all resentment disappears, regardless of how much we enjoy hanging on to resentful feelings.

Forgiving is an action verb which doesn't allow us to sit around and wait for the other person to repent. Just as Christ died for us while we were yet sinners, forgiving means we take the first step in healing a relationship.

2. *To forgive* also means: "to give up or give away." If someone violates your rights, forgiveness means you give up the right of reaction and the right to get even, no matter how much you may feel revenge is justified. To forgive means to give mercy, not to demand justice—a response which runs counter to everything our society teaches.

What if God insisted on getting even with us every time we sinned? We each would have been blown away long ago. I have never prayed to God and asked for His justice in my relationship with Him. I have always asked for mercy. And it wasn't until a couple of years ago I came to the humbling realization that one problem I had was that I was asking for mercy from God, but demanding justice in my own relationships with other people.

The world tells us to hate and God says to love. The world says we must take revenge, but God says to forgive. Why? Because the basis of our forgiveness is what Jesus Christ did on the cross for you and me. To the Colossians Paul writes, "...in whom we have redemption, the forgiveness of sin" (Colossians 1:14). This is elaborated on in Hebrews 10:10-12: "By this will we have been sanctified through the offering of the body of Jesus Christ once for all. And every priest stands daily ministering and offering time after time the same sacrifices, which can never take away sins; but He, having offered one sacrifice for sins for all time, SAT DOWN AT THE RIGHT HAND OF GOD." He offered one sacrifice for all time to forgive us.

The basis for our forgiveness is described in 1 Peter 1:18,19: "...knowing that you were not redeemed with perishable things like silver or gold...but with precious blood, as of a lamb unblemished and spotless, the blood of Christ." The very basis for God forgiving us is not something we have done, but rather who Jesus Christ is, and what He has done in our behalf on the cross. This then is our model for forgiving others.

Me Too?

The truly revolutionary part of God's forgiveness and what ours should be is found in the extent of His forgiveness. God's forgiveness is complete. As Psalm 103:12 depicts it, He put our sins "as far away as the east is from the west." Now north to south can be measured, but east to west cannot. This phrase specifically alludes to eternity. The extent of God's forgiveness is for all eternity.

Resolving conflicts in interpersonal relationships starts with resolving the conflict in our relationship with God and being forgiven by

Him. For years, however, I didn't realize that it also included me forgiving myself. I recognized God forgave me on the basis of what Jesus Christ did, but as far as I was concerned, I had to stop doing this and start doing that to earn the right to forgive myself. For the longest time it did not occur to me that forgiving myself wasn't dependent upon something I had to do but upon what Christ had already done for me on the cross. Christians need to forgive themselves, and whenever a Christian doesn't forgive himself or herself, it is dishonoring to God.

For a considerable time I lived out the pattern followed by many Christians. I would confess my sins to God, acknowledge His forgiveness, and then put myself on a guilt trip. In so doing I was by my actions implying that Jesus Christ's death on the cross was not sufficient for all my sins.

You see, the real issue at stake as we go through life is not so much how many or few times we blow it. The issue is how you and I deal with it when we do sin. For example, one day about eight of us were talking in a restaurant in the little town where I live and I made a certain statement that I never should have made because it hurt another brother there. At the time I really didn't realize what my remarks really implied, but that was no excuse.

Halfway Home

Being unaware of the problem, I said goodbye to everyone after dinner and headed home. Then all of a sudden, bam! In all of my life I have never been so convicted by the Holy Spirit. The conviction concerning the wrongness of what I had said during dinner just welled up within me. Right then I confessed it to God, but I couldn't continue driving home. I knew I had to go back and confess the sin to my brother.

So I turned around. I found him and I said, "What I said was wrong and I know I hurt you, and it was sin. I've confessed it to God, and I've come back to confess it to you and ask your forgiveness. Will you forgive me?"

To my amazement he said, "No!"

I thought I must have heard him wrong, so I tried again.

He said, "Well, you never should have said it!"

Of course if I hadn't realized that I wouldn't have returned to the restaurant! So I tried once more to explain it to him and he said, "Someone like you never should have said that." (I always get that thrown at me, "Someone like you...". I'm a person too. I put my pants on like everybody else—one leg at a time—unless I'm in a hurry.)

Now I'm sure there have been other people who wouldn't forgive me, but they didn't come right out and say it. People tend to say, "Oh, I forgive you," yet they hold a grudge against me to this day. This, however, was the first person who ever looked me in the eye and said,

"I won't forgive you."

How should one respond to that? I was at a loss for words. I was even at a loss for theological content. I got in my car and drove home and I was miserable! I started "singing to myself" what he was saying, "How could you, a staff member of Campus Crusade for Christ, say something like that? Who do you think you are? How could God use you?" I wrote a whole new hymn we could all sing in church, called, "Oh Woe Is Me." When I got home I really let myself have it, over and over again, "God can't use you!"

Suddenly I realized what was happening. I said, "Hold everything! (I talk to myself all the time) I have two choices. I can turn my back on Christ and the cross and feel sorry for myself, or I can face up to the fact that I blew it, acknowledge it to God and the man I hurt (which I had done), and get on with my life, having learned not to do again what I did."

I wish I could say my act immediately came together right then and there, but it didn't. I went on feeling sorry for myself for some time.

Do you see what I was doing? I was making forgiveness from that brother the prerequisite to me forgiving myself. I was letting someone else control my life and my relationships with my heavenly Father.

Finally, after wallowing in my unforgiveness for about half an hour, I just said, "Josh, this is stupid! You know better than this!" Then the reality struck me: the basis of me forgiving myself is Jesus Christ's death on the cross. I confessed the whole thing to God one more time for my own sake, and then I added, "Oh yes, Josh, I forgive you." With that I started "singing praises" and began to walk again by faith.

Well, my inner happiness really irritated the peace of this brother. This dynamic went on for about a year. During this time I repeatedly went out of my way to express love to him as never before. One day I evaluated the situation again and said to Dottie, "You know, the relationship has been healed. In fact, it's better now than it's ever been." And it is! The other day as I was driving out of town to go to the airport this brother charged out from a store and stopped me. We just stood there together right in the middle of the street...and almost got run over.

Because I fly a lot I have a practice of using those few minutes before a plane takes off to reminisce on the events of the day and what God has done. This time I broke into a cold sweat when I realized that if I had not made the decision to forgive myself and walk by faith, that relationship would probably never have been healed.

Think of it. Many relationships are not healed today because believers are not willing to forgive themselves. If you cannot forgive yourself, you're going to have continued conflict in the relationship. Christ's death on the cross extends to us forgiving ourselves. We need to fix our focus entirely on His actions and not our own.

Forgiveness also extends to other people. Hal Lindsay, in *The Liberation of Planet Earth*, writes, "If God has forgiven us all our sins, what should our attitude be about sin in ourselves and others? For me to fail to forgive myself or anyone else who has offended me is to imply that I have a higher standard of forgiveness than God, because whatever it is that has so hurt me that I can't forgive it, God already has."[3] In Hebrews 10:14, He teaches us, "For by that one offering He made forever perfect in the sight of God all those whom He is making holy" (TLB). You can't improve on that.

The basis of all forgiveness, whether it be forgiving ourselves or another person, is Jesus' death on the cross. An individual who refuses to forgive another person is actually cutting oneself off from God's forgiveness,

Have you ever really thought about the revolutionary statement in the Lord's Prayer? Freely translated, Jesus taught us to pray, "Lord, forgive me *as I have forgiven others*." I had recited the Lord's Prayer, our model prayer, for twenty years and yet had never realized that we ask God to forgive us only to the extent that we forgive others.

Burn No Bridges

I would encourage you to engrave this phrase across the billboard of your mind: "When I refuse to forgive, I am burning a bridge that someday I will need to pass over." No matter who you are, more often than you can imagine, you are going to need forgiveness from someone else.

Who are you and I to forgive? You must forgive anyone who has angered you, hurt you, abused you, or offended you. And you must start with your spouse. In Hosea we read that when his wife became a prostitute, he went out and bought her on the auction block, brought her home and forgave her. Not only are we to forgive our mates, we are to forgive former mates. So many divorced people seethe with bitterness from a broken relationship and will not forgive. Not only do they suffer the emotional torture of their unwillingness to forgive, but their children also suffer tremendously the most because of it.

You also need to forgive your children when they hurt you, and let the incident pass from your memory.

Many people carry bitter feelings toward a parent because of incest, divorce, abuse or alcoholism. You were not born to those parents by chance—God hand-picked them for you. No matter how bad a situation was, God can still use it for your good, and you need to forgive your parents. Not only is this biblical, but I know its value from personal experience.

You need to forgive other family members. My eldest brother Wilmot was my parents' favorite, yet when he left the farm he sued them for 50 percent of everything they owned. For years I resented him for hurting my mother so badly and for the humiliating public display he made of our family problems.

Not long after I became a Christian, God began to convict me of my bitterness toward Wilmot. So I wrote him a letter—the perfect model of how not to forgive someone. It was five pages long. The first four and nine-tenths pages listed everything he had done wrong and for which he needed forgiveness. I even added the charming statement, "You killed Mom," because I knew he had. Between my father's drunken abuse and Wilmot's lawsuit, my mother had just given up the will to live.

At the close of the last page I wrote, "I have come to know Jesus Christ personally and I want you to know I forgive you." I signed it and then tacked on this P.S.: "I never want to see you again."

Well, after forgiving someone I thought you were supposed to feel better, but I felt rotten! Finally I had to admit that I had blown it and I found myself having to seek forgiveness for the way I had forgiven (not too many people do that). I bought a postcard so that I couldn't write much. I wrote on it the simple words: "Wilmot, I forgive you and I love you. Josh." In Acts 7 we read that as Stephen was being stoned to death, he cried out, "Lord, do not hold this sin against them" (verse 60). We need to learn to forgive those who commit crimes against us.

Tough Forgiveness

Goldie Bristol didn't learn of the rape and brutal murder of her twenty-one year old daughter until she received a terse telegram from the coroner. It read: "Your daughter Diane—we have her body. How do you want it disposed of?" After the funeral, God led the family to pray for the killer. He was caught, and Goldie received permission to go to the federal prison. There she looked the man square in the face and said, "I forgive you."

We must even forgive those who have hurt our most cherished loved ones. The bride of six months of a dear brother who had worked on my staff team for several years was killed by a drunk driver. Charlie went to the man and forgave him for killing his wife, and I had to bring myself to forgive the man in my own heart.

Some of us are haunted by people who have died without our forgiveness. We need to forgive people from the past. We also need to forgive those around us who persecute us; who intimidate us; who harass, attack, and irritate us. First, we must be sure that the real problem lies with the other person and not with something we are doing. But once we recognize that we are not being treated right and we acknowledge our attitude toward those involved, then we can receive forgiveness ourselves; ask God to forgive them; and lift them up in prayer.

Our culture says, "You have rights. Demand your rights!" But God has called us to forgive those who tread upon our rights, whether they be in the area of reputation, time, finances, comfort or anything else. This includes everything from insults to criticism to rejection—everything. "I'll forgive everything *except* ..." is not true forgiveness. Forgiveness extends to our relationship with the God the Father, to ourselves and to others. It is all-encompassing and eternal.

At Peace Now

You may be asking, "When do I forgive?" Paul exhorts us in Ephesians 4:26: "Do not let the sun go down on your wrath." The Bible doesn't forbid us us to be angry, rather it exhorts us to control our anger. I believe that if you go to bed "mad," your anger is controlling you. Basically, forgiveness should be given, extended, or received *immediately*. The length of time between the hurt and the extending of our forgiveness is really an indicator of the strength of our walk with God.

When dealing with other people, you need to forgive them or ask forgiveness of them whenever it can be a help, blessing or encouragement to the other. A young man named Matt commented to his friend about some questionable dealings of a local minister. When Matt got home, he realized that his comments were out of line and called the friend. He said, "One of my biggest concerns is division within the body of Christ, and there I was saying divisive things. I'm sorry I subjected you to that, and I hope you will forgive me." His friend replied, "You know, I hadn't even given it a second thought, but you're right—you shouldn't have said that. Of course I forgive you. Thanks for bringing it up."

Sometimes, however, an immediate confession would not be an encouragement to the other person because they are not ready for it emotionally. You may need to cope with it in your own life for a few days and then deal with the other person.

Summing Up the Basis

We have three resources for forgiving. The first is our model, Jesus Christ, and His provision for forgiveness. The second is that the Holy Spirit empowers us to forgive—we cannot forgive on our own. The more we walk in the filling of the Spirit, the more forgiving we will be. Our third resource for forgiving is the guidance of the Word of God.

Then there are three areas we can focus on to help us understand forgiveness and to practice it in our daily lives. One is to recognize the depth of Christ's forgiveness. He made one sacrifice for *all* sins for *all* time. Next, try as we might, we cannot work for forgiveness. If we focus on Christ as the basis of our forgiveness, we quickly realize that we cannot earn it. In Romans 1:17 we are told we go "...from faith to faith," and I think that means we start the Christian life by faith and live it by faith. I know that I started by faith, but so often I want to live it by works.

The third focus is our own need of forgiveness. I amaze myself sometimes. Someone will do something offensive to me, and I will totally forget that I have ever been forgiven by anyone. I can be a steamroller, and with my kind of personality I have had to be forgiven far more than I will ever have to forgive. When I focus on my own need of forgiveness, it keeps forgiving others in perspective.

This Isn't Forgiveness

Forgiveness is not just saying, "Well, I'm sorry." When you do that, you are acknowledging the problem but not your responsibility for getting yourself off the hook. Forgiveness is saying, "I'm sorry. Will you forgive me?" I also like to specifically state what it is I'm seeking forgiveness for.

Forgiveness is not conditional and cannot be earned. You can't demand changes of someone, "Maybe if you clean up your life I'll forgive you." There are no strings attached to true forgiveness.

Forgiveness is not a feeling. There have been times when I sure didn't feel like forgiving and had to do it by faith. Yet I can't remember a single instance of forgiving by faith when the feelings didn't come afterward. Forgiveness is an act of the will.

Forgiveness is not keeping score. You can't make mental notes each time something occurs and you think that you are being forgiving. Paul reminds us in 1 Corinthians 13:5 that love "keeps no record of wrongs," which means you are to love the person and respond to them in the same manner as before the wrong occurred.

Forgiveness is not pretending that the situation never happened. So often people just go on with life and act as though there never was a problem. If this is how you are dealing with a situation, don't be surprised when it comes back to haunt you again.

Forgiveness is not indifference. If your attitude is "so what?" you are ignoring a conflict that needs to be dealt with. Such indifference is superficial.

Forgiveness is not condoning wrong. Just because you have resolved the personal hurt through forgiveness doesn't mean that you condone a wrong action.

Forgiveness is not just saying, "Let's forget about it." You don't forget about it. Rather, it becomes a source of irritation or resentment. Forgetting does not result in forgiveness. It's really the other way around: forgiveness results in forgetting.

Forgiveness is not tolerance. Simply forever putting up with a problem doesn't resolve anything and cannot help a relationship.

Forgiveness does not strive to teach the offender a lesson.

Forgiveness does not mean there won't be consequences. There could still be a loss of reputation, financial loss, emotional loss, loss of sleep or any number of consequences. You need to understand that a person who does wrong has a *personal* responsibility and a *legal* responsibility. If you forgive someone, that means that you have dealt with it on a personal level, but that individual still has to answer to God. You can forgive the driver with no insurance who smashed your car, but that person still has to deal with the law.

Forgiveness does not mean that the person you forgave is going to change. Whether that person changes or not, your commandment from God is to forgive; we are not responsible for another's actions.

Finally, forgiveness deals effectively with past wounds, but cannot insulate you against future hurts. If you can forgive now, however, you will be better able to deal with the conflict and hurts to come.

Intimacy in a marriage is not contingent on never offending your partner. If it were, none of our marriages would ever survive. Rather, intimacy is dependent upon your willingness to forgive and to seek forgiveness. People who quote the line from the *Love Story* theme: "Love means never having to say you're sorry," show little understanding of the nature of intimate relationships. Two people in a love relationship *will* experience conflict, but real love is always ready to forgive. Asking for forgiveness in a mature relationship will not leave you open for abuse. Instead, as when I ask Dottie's forgiveness for something, I have the assurance that she will not take advantage of my vulnerability.

This is Forgiveness

Now that we've seen what forgiveness is not, let's take a look at what forgiveness is. First off, forgiveness is an expression of strength, not weakness. More men than women are afraid that forgiving and seeking forgiveness could mean showing personal weakness in keeping up their macho image. Believe me, however, seeking to heal a relationship through forgiveness is a real sign of strength of character.

Forgiveness is an expression of love that takes the initiative. Have you ever thought, "Why should I forgive her, she hasn't sought forgiveness?" God's love, however, compels us to take the first step. In 1 John 4:10, we read, "In this is love; not that we loved God, but that He loved us and sent His Son to be the propitiation (the atoning sacrifice) for our sins" (Amplified). If God had waited for us to repent and ask His forgiveness, we would still be lost. And if you wait for another person to first confess and seek your forgiveness, you are letting that person control your life.

Jesus said, "If therefore you are presenting your offering at the altar, and there remember that your brother has something against you, leave your offering there before the alter, and go your way; first be reconciled to your brother, and then come and present your offering" (Matthew 5:23,24). Here God clearly explains that He wants you to take the initiative, no matter who needs forgiveness—He doesn't even want you to worship if there is a relationship you haven't tried to make right. If people were to follow this biblical instruction and to stay away from church because they refused to seek or offer forgiveness, I wonder how many would show up next Sunday morning?

Forgiveness has three objectives in view. The first is seen in the words of Jesus we just looked at. It is *reconciliation* between two individuals. The second objective is found in Colossians 3:12-15: "And let the peace of Christ rule in your hearts, to which indeed you were called into one body, and be thankful." Forgiveness promotes *unity in the body of Christ*. A third objective is *emotional healing*— one of the greatest ways the healing love of Jesus Christ can be demonstrated to a watching world.

Why Don't We Forgive?

Now to better understand how we can apply forgiveness in our lives, let's take a look at some of the reasons why you and I don't forgive.

Insecurity is certainly one of those reasons. If you or I feel insecure with ourselves or in our relationship with God, we are going to look for every opportunity to be assertive. Getting "one up" on someone by not forgiving them can provide a certain false sense of security.

Holding a grudge is another reason we don't forgive. In Ephesians 4:30 and 32 we are instructed not to harbor bitterness, yet we all know there is a kind of pleasure to be taken in such resentment.

Several years ago I spoke at Cal-Poly, Pomona, California, on the revolution of love. After my talk, a black woman came up to me. (I mention that she was black because blacks in our culture have so many more sources for bitterness and resentment than any white person ever will. Most whites can't even begin to identify with the frustrations and injustices blacks experience.) She said, "You know, Mr. McDowell, I really appreciated what you shared today, but I would not want the love for people that you have for me."

That really hit me! "Why not?" I asked.

"Because," she said, "I want the joy of hating those who hate me!"

Some people are motivated for a lifetime by bitterness. Some of the most well-known events of history were perpetrated because of a grudge. One reason we don't forgive is because we relish harboring "the right to resentment."

Jealousy is another frequent reason we don't forgive. King Saul's hatred for David was rooted in jealousy, and we don't want to forgive someone who has something we think we should have. When someone is better off than we may be, we basically decide they don't deserve our forgiveness.

Fear is actually another major reason people don't forgive. When you forgive someone, you see, you make yourself vulnerable. You might not forgive another person because you have been burned before and are afraid of being hurt again. This is where the health of own your self-image comes in. Until you see yourself as God sees you—no more and no less—you will not be willing to lay yourself open. But, when you offer to heal the relationship, you have acted rightly in the sight of God, whether that person accepts or rejects your offer.

Self-pity can keep us from forgiving. "Oh, I've been hurt more than anyone, and I just can't forgive anymore!" is this person's argument. But, Romans 8:28 assures us that God works all things (even the bad ones) together for the good, and in self-pitying, we put our judgement above God's. We say in effect: "God, this area cannot work together for the good, and You are powerless to do anything about it."

Shifting the blame is another frequent cop-out for not forgiving. The feeling that "I was in the right, and I had a right to do what I did" has kept untold numbers of people from experiencing forgiveness and has destroyed countless relationships.

Plain old madness at a person will keep you from forgiving. You really don't mind if someone does what he did to you to someone else, but how dare he do it to you! Ephesians 4:26 tells us: "Do not let the sun go down on your wrath." And please note that this is a commandment, not merely a suggestion.

Pride is another response that will ward off forgiveness. Pride says: "I don't need this relationship; I don't need that person."

Failing to forget is yet another reason you will not forgive. Forgetting doesn't just mean the inability to recall a situation. I believe forgetting means that you disregard or push aside the event, refusing to get so hung up on yesterday's hurts that you miss today's joys.

If you're into cars, think of forgetting as not getting all of the mileage due out of something. Or if you were raised on a farm, like me, think about forgetting as not milking a situation for all it's worth. Forgetting means not keeping a scorecard of wrongs. To forget means to put it on the shelf and let it gather dust. And when a similar situation comes along you can take a look on the shelf and remind yourself of what not to do, and then put it out of your mind again. *To forget means to no longer be controlled by the hurt or the desire to get even.*

When I study a topic, God usually takes the opportunity to make in-course corrections in my walk with Him. While studying on forgiveness, I found out what I was doing wrong and what I was doing right. God encouraged me in what I was doing right and convicted me in those areas that needed correcting.

Now when situations pop up, I can look on the shelf where I've put past hurts, learn something from them, and say, "That was wrong, but Christ died for that." Then I put it back on the shelf and walk by faith—better able to cope with future hurts. That is how God is at work to make me a better person.

Henry Ward Beecher explains that the phrase, "I can forgive, but I cannot forget" is only another way of saying, "I cannot forgive."

Unworthiness is still another reason we don't forgive. We decide the person doesn't deserve to be forgiven. The Bible, however, hasn't given you or me the option of that judgement. It says, "Forgive." Period! What did you do to deserve Christ's forgiveness?

The repeat offender is another classic reason for failing to forgive. "I've already forgiven you five times, so I'm not going to forgive you again. If I forgive you again, you'll just go do it again, and that makes the whole thing cheap." I have actually felt this way toward a brother, thinking he needed to be taught a lesson before I would forgive him again. By freely forgiving again and again we underscore the limitless forgiveness God offers us through Christ. But knowing that God will forgive us doesn't imply that we should willfully sin. It just means that when we do blow it, God forgives us and takes us back without reservation.

In Christ's time, the consensus among rabbis was that you forgave a man four times and no more. Some of the more generous teachers may have gone as high as seven times, but that was considered radical. Can you imagine then the scene when Peter asks Jesus how often he should forgive his brother? Peter expects to really impress Jesus with his spirituality and willingness to forgive by going out on a religious limb and offering, "Up to seven times?"

You can almost see Peter with his chest out and a satisfied smile on his face, waiting for Jesus to pat him on the back and say, "Oh no, Peter! I really appreciate the depth of your spirituality, but two or three times is plenty!"

Instead, Jesus turns to Peter and says, "I do not say to you, up to seven times, but up to seventy times seven." Can't you then just hear Peter stammering to respond: "Uh, Lord, You want to run that by me again? Did you say 490 times?" Jesus isn't interested in the number; He's interested in a forgiving attitude and a boundless desire to heal relationships. This goes against everything the world teaches, and denies us the option of demanding our rights after two or three hurts. Our natural reaction is to give up on someone after a few tries. We have to reach out in forgiveness by faith, even when we don't want to.

Revenge is sometimes our motive when we don't want to forgive. We simply want to see that person fail in an important project or relationship. We want to cause suffering in that life equal to or worse than what that person has caused in our own. But the Bible instructs, "Never pay back evil for evil to anyone. Respect what is right in the sight of all men. If possible, so far as it depends on you, be at peace with all men" (Romans 12:17,18). God says in Hebrews 10:30, "Vengeance is Mine, I will repay."

A lack of strength is a final reason we don't forgive. After a deep hurt, we simply may feel we are not emotionally strong enough to say sincerely, "I forgive you."

The Irresistible Force

Corrie ten Boom with her sister, whom she loved and greatly admired, were prisoners in Hitler's Ravensbruk concentration camp. One guard was exceptionally brutal to them. Corrie could handle being treated badly, but she could hardly bear to see this guard being so cruel to her sister who eventually died from the beatings. Over the years, a great resentment toward this German guard built up inside Corrie.

After the war, Corrie went to Germany not just to say a message of forgiveness, but to *be* a message of forgiveness. Guilt was heavy on the German people, and they were silent as they came in and out of the church where she was speaking. One of the people standing in line to greet her after the service was the guard who had beaten her sister. He did not recognize her, and said, "I was a guard in a prison camp, and I appreciated your message tonight. I have come to know Jesus Christ as my Savior and Lord, and I have come to you because I need your forgiveness."

Here Corrie had just delivered a talk on forgiveness. Yet when she recognized the man as the one who had so cruelly abused her sister, bitterness boiled inside of her. He did not realize who he was talking to and stood there with his hand out. But Corrie could not raise her arm to take it. He repeated, "Corrie, will you forgive me?" Within herself she cried out, "Oh, God, help me!" and suddenly she felt a warmth come through her body. Before she realized what she was doing, she had taken his hand, was looking him in the eye and saying, "I forgive you."

God has often brought to my mind this episode in Corrie ten Boom's life, just when I needed to reach out in faith and forgive. I can't explain it exactly, but the power to forgive will always come if you will let it. The Holy Spirit is there when we are weak to give us sufficient strength to forgive anything.

Giving and receiving forgiveness is the greatest power available for resolving conflicts today. It is one of the greatest needs in all the world. Showing to the world Christ's character by being a forgiving person is one of the most powerful testimonies you or I can give.

I have often prayed a prayer asking God to make me a more forgiving person. It goes like this: "Heavenly Father, thank You for forgiveness. Thank You for Jesus Christ dying on the cross for my sins, that I might be totally forgiven. Thank You that when I placed my faith in Christ, my sins were forgiven because of what He has done, and not something I did. Father, show me how to forgive myself and those around me. I want to forgive as You do, and I want to take the initiative to offer forgiveness. Give me the strength to swallow my pride and seek forgiveness when I have done wrong. Heal me of all resentful feelings.

"Lord, I ask for conviction when I need conviction, healing when I need healing, irritation when I need irritation, and comfort when I need comfort. Let me be a channel of Your forgiveness to the world. In Jesus's name, amen."

Questions to Ponder

- Why is forgiveness the basis of lasting, intimate relationships?
- What can we do to understand forgiveness and practice it in our own lives?
- What are some reasons we don't forgive?
- What does the Bible say about forgiveness?

FURTHER HELPFUL RESOURCES:
Richard P. Walters, *Forgive & Be Free*, (Grand Rapids, MI: Zondervan Publishing House, 1983).
Dr. David Augsburger, *Caring Enough To Forgive*, (Ventura, CA: Regal Books, 1981).
Dr. David Augsburger, *The Freedom Of Forgiveness*, (Chicago, IL: Moody Press, 1970).
Goldie Bristol With Carol McGinnis, *When It's Hard To Forgive*, (Wheaton, IL: Victor Books, 1982).
Josh McDowell, *His Image ... My Image* (Here's Life Publishers).
Jeanette Lockerbie, *Forgive, Forget and Be Free* (Here's Life Publishers).

CHAPTER ———————— 8

BECOMING TRUSTWORTHY

What would you say is the overriding concern in your life as a woman? As a man?

Studies show that men put significance at the top of their scale of values. If a wife belittles a man in any way and chips at his significance, she can expect either withdrawal or anger.

Women, on the other hand, value security. They need the security of an adequate supply of money, of a safe environment. Yet more than anything else a wife needs the security of being able to trust her husband. When she is sure of that she will take the pressure off in many areas.

Strangely, being trustworthy is a character strength that does not receive much emphasis these days. Yet trustworthiness is the basis for an enduring and intimate love, marriage, and sexual relationship.

A Shared Identity

To achieve intimacy a couple must have a shared identity—a "we" relationship. A couple must strive for honesty and openness and allow themselves to be vulnerable. Without the trust factor, there can be no honesty and closeness.

A friend sensed that his wife was being physically and emotionally attracted to a man with whom she was working. He went out of his way to express his love for her, to help her in difficult situations, and to let her know he really cared about her. Relaxed in her husband's unconditional love and commitment to her as his wife, she trusted him enough to share her inner turmoil. Instead of condemning her, he assured her of his support in prayer as she attempted to sort out her feelings. Over several weeks they were able to develop a new relationship of love and trust so strong the potential intruder was sidelined.

Now if you do not have the confidence that your spouse is faithful, trustworthy, and always thinking the best of you and for you, it is almost impossible to be open and develop an intimate and lasting relationship. You may be living in the same house, but you both will be intensely lonely.

Commenting on such loneliness, Richard Strauss writes, "Loneliness is an awful thing. It is emptiness, incompleteness, lack of communion, lack of personal companionship. Loneliness is the lack of opportunity to share yourself with someone who understands—someone with whom you can enjoy a mutual commitment and trust."[1]

Like character, trust is not the product of a series of one-night stands. It is developed over an extended period of time. And more people are becoming aware of the need to build trust into a relationship, especially when they hope to develop one that is meaningful.

One student confessed, "Most of the time, when I found myself in bed with someone, I wished it never had gotten that far. After I reached a point where I knew I would wind up spending the night with her, it was all downhill. I just went through the motions. There were times when all I wanted was to hurry up and get it over with. I finally stopped messing around when I realized that sex is no good unless there is a true trust and love involved. Without it, it's just not worth the hassle."[2]

Lonnie Barbech, a social psychologist, and Linda Levine, a psychotherapist, have observed in their counseling sessions that trustworthiness is a factor that allows freedom and leads to commitment: "Women in secure, caring relationships say that they feel less self-conscious, more able to lose themselves in a sensual experience, because they trust their partners and feel accepted by them."[3]

I believe trustworthiness is simply a reflection of what we are like deep down inside and what we have proven ourselves to be. And it takes time to build this quality into our character.

Freedom Requires Trust

It is obvious that the trust factor is vitally important in the area of the physical. If you can learn to control your sex life before marriage, you will be able to control it in marriage. Waiting until marriage to have sex increases mutual trust. God's design for sex involves a one hundred percent abandonment to only your mate. It doesn't take long to realize that if there is any distrust in the relationship, intimacy, closeness and total abandonment to one's mate is extremely difficult to achieve.

One man in Indiana had lost his wife in an auto accident, and after a few years he began to date again. Finally he fell in love and planned to remarry. But for reasons beyond their control they had to wait nearly two years. Although he had known the pleasure of sex within a marriage, he never did anything more than kiss her goodbye during this waiting period.

After they were married, the woman beamed with pride at his behavior. She said, "There were times when it would have been so easy to just let nature take its course, but he never let his guard down. There is no one in the world I trust more than my husband. He is gone a lot on business, but I would trust him if he were the only man on a tropical island with 500 naked women." His self control paid off in their marriage.

Building a Foundation

As a single person, I never realized how much my dating life would eventually affect my relationship with my wife. No one ever shared with me that my dating experiences would directly influence the joy and happiness of my marriage. I dated a young lady by the name of Paula when I was in graduate school. We dated for three and a half years and almost got married. Even though we were very compatible, and enjoyed and respected each other immensely, the fullness of a love given by God was missing. We finally broke up and continued to be the closest of friends.

Three years later I met Dottie, and not long after we were married, Dottie met Paula. They became good friends and started spending a lot of time together. Eventually, Paula moved close to our home in California, where her parents and sister also live. We practically became neighbors.

One morning I arrived home from a trip and Dottie wasn't there. When she returned she told me she had spent the morning with Paula. She came over, put her arms around me and said, "Honey, I'm sure glad you behaved yourself for three and a half years."

I took a deep breath and asked hesitantly, "Why?"

Dottie responded, "Paula shared with me this morning that she was so in love with you that there were times she would have done anything for you, but you never once took advantage of her." Needless to say, there was a big sigh of relief from me, and I was profoundly glad I had never pushed Paula in the area of the physical.

A Great Track Record

Can you imagine what that conversation with Paula meant to my wife? It affirmed: "I can trust my husband!" In a recent interview, Dottie shared this: "You must build your relationship on trust. I trust Josh to be a good provider for my children. I trust him to be faithful to me. I trust him to be our spiritual leader and to have his own relationship with Christ. And I trust him as a person who is going to take care of our finances.

"He can trust me to be a good mother while he's gone. He can trust me with feeding the children properly and nutritiously. As he travels he can trust me not to be spending lots of money or having wild parties. Everything you do, every step you take in a relationship together, has to be built on trust. It is the foundation for your marriage. It is easy to abandon yourself to someone when you trust him.

"If I ever had a serious problem, who would I go to? Immediately I think that I would go to a person I trust, someone who loves me for who I am, and who is not going to change his opinion about me regardless of what I have done. And Josh is that person, because I totally trust him. The reason I trust him is because he has a trustworthy track record. He has made hard choices, and even as a non-Christian those choices were good. He has always had high moral standards.

"For anybody who has had a problem in the past, I think communication is the most important step. A couple needs to let each other know that there is trust in spite of the past."

As you become trustworthy, you will also find yourself to be more trusting of others. Paul emphasized this aspect of love when he wrote, "Love shows no end of its trust" (1 Corinthians 13:7, Phillips).

Mature love has a faith which cannot be destroyed. To a person who has repeatedly made mistakes, love is ready to believe again. Christ is our greatest model of that type of love. He is always ready to love anew. Christ always believes the best, and if He is let down one thousand times, He remains ready to forgive and trust again the one thousand and first time.

Questions to Ponder

● In what ways is trust the basis for a lasting marriage relationship?
● Why is trust important in the area of the physical?

FURTHER HELPFUL RESOURCES:
Alan McGinnis, *The Friendship Factor* (Augsbury).
Jerry White, *Friends and Friendship* (Nav).

9

RESPONDING TO AUTHORITY

You will be the right person and a better marriage partner if you develop a natural and proper response to authority while you are single. A positive response to authority in your life is vital to a successful marriage relationship.

If you are the kind of person who always has to have his own way—who rebelled against parents, employers or teachers—you will have a difficult time developing a close and intimate relationship. The individual who habitually rejects authority will find it difficult to respond to his or her mate in a positive way.

In a marriage, two people come together from different backgrounds and with different habits. They have different likes and dislikes. They purpose to make a union which is first a strong marriage bond and later a strong family bond. Because few of life's assignments require more flexibility than marriage, a proper response to authority is essential. If one of the partners has not learned this response, the conflict will be accentuated.

While living in Latin America a number of years ago, I learned some important lessons about authority. At times I would not feel at peace with a certain decision, either because of a personal preference or a cultural difference. But I learned that, even though I thought something should be done my way, I needed to respond to the authority of the Argentines and go along with their decision. God taught me the lesson of doing what someone else wanted me to do, even when I thought my idea was better, or when I simply didn't want to do it their way. What a great preparation for marriage! If you have learned to not always have it your way, you are better able to respond to your mate in marriage.

A Yellow Kitchen

Let me illustrate how this lesson has paid off in my relationship with my wife. The dream of having our own home had come true when we moved into a nice Spanish-style house. It wasn't very expensive, but it took every penny we had. I thought it was immaculate.

We moved in and unpacked and before the dust could settle, my wife said, "Honey, could we paint the kitchen?" Personally, I thought the kitchen looked great! It had kind of a dirty mustard yellow color, but the paint wasn't peeling. I told her I really didn't think it needed painting, but she said, "Please, I'd really like to have it a different color of yellow."

Then I started to think about it. Painting the kitchen meant a lot to my wife, even though I couldn't have cared less. After all, she was probably going to spend more time there than I would. And this is where I had to respond to authority. Although we really didn't have much money, I realized that painting the kitchen was the best investment of the money we did have. It would demonstrate to my wife that I cared about her wants and desires, so I decided to start painting.

Now I didn't say to my wife, "Fine, I'll do it, just get off my back!" That would have robbed us both of the joy. Instead I said, "Okay, honey, let's paint it," and I went to work. After I had the first coat on I had to admit the previous color really had been an ugly mustard yellow color. The second coat finally produced the desired results and left the wall a warm, bright yellow.

My wife came in and admired my work—she made me feel like a king—and when she was finished admiring, I felt like I had painted the Sistine kitchen. Then she asked, "Honey, could we trim it in white?" Since I used to own a painting company, I knew exactly what she was asking me to do. I knew how difficult it would be to paint the trim. But I got up early the next morning, put on another coat and painted the trim. I could hardly wait for my wife to see it. I remember our first meal in the kitchen after I had finished. Dottie put her arms around me and said, "Honey, I know you didn't want to paint, but it meant a lot to me. Thank you so much."

Can you imagine what this meant to Dottie? She couldn't help but feel like, "He cares! He cares about my desires, my wants and my needs!" We reaped tremendous benefits from this experience. Giving and taking and responding to each other's authority is absolutely necessary in an intimate relationship of oneness.

Ammons and Stinnett are a couple of researchers who have studied vital marriages. A key characteristic of happy married partners is that they "are sensitive to other people...they recognize the needs of others, respect their differences, consider their feelings, put themselves in the other person's shoes."[1] After a study of 2,500 married persons, Dr. Lewis Terman describes the person likely to be happy in marriage this way: "He is cooperative in his attitude toward other people. *He works well with those in authority over him.* [Italics mine.] He is kind and sympathetic toward his inferiors, and always ready to help anyone in trouble."

Furthermore, Terman explains, "By contrast, here is the person likely to be an unhappy marriage partner. He is not sure of himself in social relationships, and usually feels inferior. When he finds himself in a superior position, however, he tends to be 'bossy' and domineering. He doesn't like taking orders from others and hates to be involved in competition because he is a bad loser. He tends to be negative, to be a chronic complainer, and to be 'agin' all authority."[2]

To Be Right or To Be Loved

One of the greatest love passages ever written speaks of responding to the desires of the loved one: "Love does not insist on its own way" (1 Corinthians 13:5, Phillips).

There is a great emphasis today on "rights." "I have my rights and I am going to insist on them," is a position commonly heard. This attitude strikes at the very heart of love and intimacy because it makes it so difficult for people to consider someone else's needs first. The apostle Paul discussed the issue of rights and duties in 1 Corinthians 7:3,4: "Let the husband fulfill his duty to his wife, and likewise also the wife to her husband. The wife does not have authority over her own body, but the husband does; and likewise also the husband does not have authority over his own body, but the wife does."

Paul emphasized this again when he wrote, "Let each of you esteem and look upon and be concerned for not [merely] his own interests, but also each for the interest of others" (Philippians 2:4, Amplified).

In *Pitfalls of Romantic Love,* author H. G. Zerof asks, "How important is being right to you? Have you learned to allow your companion his or her feelings, even though you disagree, perhaps even violently, with the opinion expressed?"[3]

The beauty of each partner responding to the desires and needs of the loved one is seen in the resulting healthy give-and-take relationship so necessary for finding fulfillment in love, marriage and sex. And the key to developing this give-and-take relationship is sensitivity and a willingness to compromise.

Dottie remembers when we were on our honeymoon in Mexico, I wanted to see a movie. She was less than thrilled with the idea, since she spoke no Spanish. Also, the movie was showing in an outdoor theater, which meant there would be bugs, and Dottie hates bugs. But I was so enthusiastic about seeing the movie that she gave in. It occurred to her, probably for the first time, that in marriage we must be willing to compromise and not always insist on having things our way. There will be differences of opinion, and times when one person needs to step aside and let the other person's happiness come before one's own.

Entertainment is an area in which we have had to adapt and learn to respond to each other. Our tastes are radically different. As Dottie explains: "The type of movies and television programs Josh likes are westerns, espionage stories and murder mysteries. On the other hand, I like love stories, people stories—anything about relationships. Oftentimes he will talk me into seeing a certain movie when I would rather see something else. However, he has taken me all the way to San Francisco several times to see a ballet, which is a wonderful step for him, because he would never go to a ballet on his own.

"A marriage has to be a 'give and take' relationship. Sometimes you may feel like you are the one doing all the giving, and other times you feel like you are doing all the taking. It generally balances out."

Another area in which our tastes differed when we got married was in sports. The only sport Dottie dearly loved and followed was baseball. She is a Red Sox fan. She married a man who watches any sport and any team—except baseball. I'm a Dallas Cowboys fan. My wife did not grow up in a home where football was a priority. She finally decided to learn about football, and I developed an interest in baseball. We made the choice not to withdraw and go our own way, but to try to find a mutual solution that would benefit us both.

Equals in Compromise

David Bogard, after having been married to the same woman for forty-seven years, wrote this: "I have also seen spruce trees which at a distance looked like one tree, but when I drew near, I could see that there were two trunks, virtually equal in diameter, each adapting and surrendering to the other, giving the impression of being one tree, but being in truth still two equal trees. Two people, joined in marriage, can so adjust to each other that neither loses what is vital, thus building a life in which two personalities, each unique, must both be given opportunity to develop without doing violence to the other. There must be give and take, each ceaselessly adjusting to the other, yet retaining what is distinctive in himself. If anyone thinks this is a simple endeavor, he is in for a rude shock."[4]

Questions to Ponder

- What does it mean to "respond to authority" in a positive way?
- Why is this important in a marriage relationship?
- How can you learn to respond to authority?

FURTHER HELPFUL RESOURCES:
Martin L. Jones, *Authority* (Banner of Truth).
Jerram Barrs, *Shepherds and Sheep* (Inter Varsity Press).

CHAPTER 10

ABOUT THOSE SKELETONS

These days it might considered laughable to talk about having a clear conscience. But if you desire to be the right person in a love and marriage relationship, having a clear conscience from the past will be basic. Beginning now to build this quality into your life and personal relationships will allow you to reap incredibly rich dividends in your marriage and love life. It is a great feeling to enter into a love, marriage and sexual relationship with a clear conscience—knowing that you have been honoring God with your life, rather than using people for your own satisfaction.

Over the years it takes time for us to grow up and learn about building relationships, and we each develop certain behavior patterns. These determine the way we typically respond to and treat other people. A good love life, then, is largely the result of a history of good relationships. Without special intervention, the way we have treated people in the past will be the same way we treat them in the present. It determines the way we will treat them in the future. This is why it is so important to practice healthy dating patterns and relationships. You are laying the groundwork for a lifelong marriage relationship.

If you have built into your life a pattern of using people for your own pleasure, you will not generally change in your marriage, no matter how sincere your feelings of love. Your dating experiences go right with you into marriage. A ceremony doesn't magically change anything. The quality of your love life will be a reflection of the quality of your character. And your character was not and is not built overnight.

Two Guiding Principles

What would you say is the dating single's Golden Rule? Here's how I express it: I will treat a woman or a man on a date the same way I want someone to treat the man or woman I will some day marry. After I became a Christian I made that my guiding principle.

How are you treating the person you are dating? Is it the way you want someone to treat the person you are going to marry? Or have you been dishonest in your relationship, the way you want someone to be dishonest with the person you are going to marry? Are you leading someone on, the way you would like someone to lead on the individual you will some day marry?

I find that most people today readily justify to themselves physical involvement before marriage. However, as Herbert J. Miles points out in his book, *Sexual Understanding Before Marriage*: "To believe logically in premarital sexual intercourse, a man must defend the right of any man to have had sexual intercourse with his mother before she was married. He must defend the right of any man to have sexual intercourse with his sister before she is married. He must defend the right of any man to have sexual intercourse with his daughter before she is married."[1]

If we can't defend one type of premarital sex, how can we say that another kind is okay? It doesn't make sense, and our consciences know it. Those who defend premarital sex on the grounds that "It's O.K. if you're in love" are simply revealing how little they understand love. Can you honestly love someone while causing them to enter into a lifelong marriage commitment with a guilty conscience? I have always wanted to be able to look my daughters squarely in the eye and tell them I hope the men they date and the men they marry will treat them the same way I treated their mother.

Another guiding principle I adopted was to conduct my dating life in such a way that I would look forward to my wife meeting my former dates. Today I am glad I stuck to that philosophy. The woman I dated for over three years and almost married has now become one of my wife's closest friends.

Hold it, you may be saying, I've not exactly been a paragon of virtue. What do I do now? Suffer? Forget marriage? No, that's not what a forgiving God expects. There is no need for the guilt to be carried over into a new relationship. Sometimes the only way to develop a clear conscience is to go back in time and to ask forgiveness for your past mistakes.

In his book *Your Life Together,* Elof G. Nelson discusses how problems can be caused by guilt feelings: "Repeatedly, people who bring me their deepest problems relate how they are still being haunted by the shame and guilt of past mistakes. While they know they are forgiven by God, there seems to be no surgery for the removal of personal emotional scars. We need, therefore, to remind ourselves that we live in daily forgiveness, understanding that we are justified by grace through faith in God. Past mistakes are forgiven by a gracious

God, and the personal recognition of forgiveness can be appropriated by renewed faith in ourselves. Christian life is sustained by the fact of forgiveness, for the reality of forgiveness is the foundation of Christian life."[2]

In addition to asking and accepting God's forgiveness for your past, you must truly forgive and accept yourself. Since you cannot change the past, be thankful that this part of your life is over and that God has the power and wants to make everything about you new in your Christian life. You can develop a clear conscience no matter how wrong you may now feel a past experience was.

Chasing Skeletons

A lot of couples come to me for counseling after they have become emotionally involved, and the one question that comes up again and again is, "How much of my past do I share with the person I love?" This issue causes tremendous agony for many. My advice is not to feel compelled to "tell all." If you know you are loved and accepted for who you are now, then your love is secure. However, if events in your past could cause either of you to question the relationship, you are on shaky ground.

A young man named Chris found himself struggling with this question. After listening to his story, I suggested he not share some of his apparent mistakes with his fiancée, *unless* his motive for the silence was fear—fear that revealing his past would negatively affect the relationship and her love and acceptance of him. If this was his real reason for withholding the information, I would counsel him to share his past with her and to let their love be tested. If the fear was there, he would never feel able to open up to her completely, and it would continue to haunt him.

David Mace, in *Getting Ready For Marriage*, gives some more insight into this area, "I offer you a simple rule about confessions. If you feel you must make them, and you are quite sure you can do so in a loving way that won't cause distress to your partner, go ahead. But if you are in doubt about it, follow this plan. Go first and make the confession in full to someone you respect and trust, and discuss whether it would be good to make the confession to the one you plan to marry. If the decision on which you both agree is not to do so, you should find that the matter won't worry you any further. You have shown your willingness to tell, and that is what matters most. If at some later time the facts should come out, and your marriage partner asks you why you didn't confess before, your reply is that you were quite willing to do so, and that you have in fact told someone (whom you could name). You then explain that you withheld the confession from your partner, because it seemed at the time to be the most loving thing to do."[3]

Remember this, a clear conscience is like having a clean and properly prepared canvas surface upon which God is to paint the masterful painting He wishes your life to be. If the surface is dirty or the images left by a previous artist aren't blotted out, the painting will have great difficulty being all that is visualized in the mind of the Master Artist.

Questions to Ponder

- What is the skeleton in your life that Satan uses to oppress you?
- How can you get rid of this skeleton?

11

NOURISH YOUR SPIRIT

Your personal relationship with God directly affects your capacity to discover and sustain a fulfilled love, marriage and sexual relationship. So one of the most vital requirements for being the "right person" must be to have a mature and growing spiritual life.

I was once asked by a frustrated husband, "What is the most important factor in a successful marriage?" I replied that in my marriage to Dottie the single most important aspect is my personal relationship with Jesus Christ. He seemed rather perplexed by that response. So I pointed out that any man and woman who draw closer together spiritually with the right attitudes will have a better sex life. This is true for Christians and non-Christians alike, because a tremendous parallel exists between spiritual intimacy and sexual enjoyment.

When Christ is at work in your heart, you begin to see people as God sees them. God regarded man important enough for Him to send His Son to the cross for man's sins. Once we accept that evaluation of our mate's significance it will make a vast difference in our life—a Christian believes that every person has genuine *value*. Thus a person is viewed not primarily as a sex object, but as someone who is to be treated with dignity and respect because God has invested eternal value in that person. Internalized, these convictions help re-program in a most positive way your most important sex organ—your mind.

Researching the Spiritual

Does hard scientific research support my position? Let's examine the results of several studies.

Two social scientists, Dr. Paul Ammons, assistant professor of Social Work and Child and Family Development at the University of Georgia, and Dr. Nick Stinnett, professor and chairman of the Department of Human Development and The Family, College of Home Economics, at the University of Nebraska, have studied what type of people have the best family relationships, including the happiest marriages. One key trait common to these families was that "they are deeply spiritual."[1]

Drs. Lorna and Philip Sarrel, sex therapists and faculty members of Yale University School of Medicine, surveyed 26,000 men and women for a report on female sexuality. The results showed a close parallel "between the strength of a woman's religious feelings and her ability to enjoy sexual experiences." They concluded that "women with the strongest positive feelings about religion tend to have very good sex lives." The highest rate of unsatisfactory sexual relationships, in fact, showed up among women who said they were "anti-religious." Thus "the women with strong feelings against religion were the likeliest to have unhappy sexual relationships."[2]

McCall's magazine survey of readers regarding intimate relationships between men and women showed that "believing women—those aware of the presence of God in their lives—often seem less inhibited, warmer and more open than others."[3]

Then, two professors from the Virginia Polytechnic Institute and State University, Michael J. Sporakowski and George A. Hughston, have interviewed couples married fifty or more years to discover what they felt were the most important factors in happy marriages. One of the tasks of the persons interviewed was to "tell what would go into [their] prescription for a happy marriage." Both husbands and wives ranked the importance of religion in the top five, with women citing it as the number one criterion for a happy marriage, rating it even higher than love![4]

In an exclusive interview, family medicine specialist Dr. Robert B. Taylor was asked if religion was important in helping a marriage develop. Dr. Taylor replied "...couples who are actively religious tend to have more stable marriages."[5]

Reporting on the work of two researchers, Dr. Nick Stinnett and Dr. John Defrain (both at the University of Nebraska) in their National Study of Family Strengths, David Milofsky writes in Redbook magazine, "One striking element of the Family Strengths Study was the high degree of religious orientation among the families who participated. Most, though not all, went to a church or synagogue regularly, participated in other church activities and had regular family prayer or Bible-reading sessions.

"Stinnett points to other research conducted over the past fifty years that found a strong correlation between religion and success and happiness in all phases of life, not just family happiness. It is not surprising, then, that a shared religious life would provide a base of common values and a sense of purpose within the family. Stinnett's point is that although the Family Strengths Study does not indicate that a belief in God is a prerequisite for family happiness or mean that non-religious families will fail to be happy, it is clear that religion can be a major source of strength for families just as for individuals."[6]

"It is no accident," writes sociologist Dr. Evelyn Duvall, "as studies have shown, that couples married in church stay together in greater numbers than those married by a civil authority; they share the common goals and values of their religion."[7]

A Chicago Tribune report on a survey of sexual preferences of 100,000 readers of *Redbook* magazine reveals, "With notable consistency, the greater the intensity of a woman's religious convictions, the likelier she is to be highly satisfied with the sexual pleasures of marriage." The report went on to acknowledge that "the greater sexual pleasure for the religious woman may be simply a manifestation of an overall greater happiness with life in general."[8]

Spirituality and Sexuality

Why do deep religious convictions have such a positive influence on love, marriage and sexual relationships? Sociologist Dr. Herbert J. Miles, in *Sexual Understanding Before Marriage*, provides the answer: "There are three lines of thought that may throw light on this question. In the first place, it is our opinion that basic Christian principles are conducive to good sex life. In human interpersonal relationships, Christianity teaches (1) that worth and values reside in persons..., (2) that we should have respect for the rights of all persons, (3) that we should be characterized by unselfish sacrifice, (4) that we should show kindness and understanding towards others, (5) that we should be tolerant, slow to judge or criticize, (6) that we should be concerned about the happiness and well-being of others, (7) that we should bear one another's burdens, and (8) that we should practice self-discipline and self-control. It is immediately obvious that these Christian concepts are the foundation principles necessary for good sexual adjustment.

"On the other hand, there are certain human traits that tend to block good sex life, such as (1) selfishness, (2) impatience, (3) unconcern for the needs and rights of others, (4) quickness to blame or to condemn, (5) unwillingness to learn, and (6) the determination to satisfy the desires of the moment. It is immediately obvious that these are non-Christian traits. Truly it can be said that basic Christian ideals are the key to both a happy marriage and a satisfying sex life.

"In the second place, our research seems to indicate that Christianity tends to make possible good sexual adjustment in marriage. Out of the one hundred and fifty-one couples in our study, ninety-eight percent were church members, eighty-three percent of husbands and ninety-six percent of wives had attended Sunday school regularly in childhood and youth, seventy-six percent of husbands and seventy-nine percent of wives had been Sunday school teachers, seventy-three percent had regularly given a tenth of their income into their church, eighty-six percent read from the Bible and prayed audibly together on their wedding night, ninety percent practiced regular family worship, ninety percent had prayer before meals, and ninety-six percent of husbands and ninety-three percent of wives led public prayer in church activities.

"It is probably safe to generalize that ninety to ninety-five percent of the members of the sample were active, consecrated Christian individuals. Let us point out that in the marriage of these Christian couples, seventy-eight percent adjusted sexually within a week, twelve percent adjusted in two months, while six percent had adjusted only at the end of thirty months. After the couples had been married six months to one year, ninety-six percent of the women who had adjusted sexually stated that their attempts to experience orgasm succeeded all of the time or most of the time.

"Also, during this same period, forty-one percent of the couples indicated that husband and wife had orgasms together all of the time or most of the time, and thirty-eight percent had orgasms together some of the time. This rate of adjustment is superior to the adjustment rate of other studies. If living a Christian life tends to block good sexual adjustment in marriage, how do we explain the high rate of adjustment of the members of our study?...Although we cannot be positive, there seems to be a relation in our study between Christian values and motivations and sexual adjustment in marriage. There is certainly no evidence here that Christian values and motivations block good sexual adjustment.

"Some writers, critical of Christianity, imply that young people committed to Christian ideals cannot talk objectively about sex in planning marriage. Our research indicates that this theory is false. Ninety-one percent of the couples revealed that they discussed frankly together personal attitudes and rather complete details about sex before their marriage. Ninety-seven percent had so discussed sex one month before marriage.

"In the third place, often many false ideas about sex are charged to Christianity when these ideas are really opposite of the Judeao-Christian teaching about sex. To illustrate, a couple, both thirty years old, the parents of three children, were separated and about to secure a divorce. Mrs. X, the mother of the wife, visited the family pastor to request his help in avoiding the divorce. In exploring the possible causes of the conflict between the couple, the pastor finally inquired if the couple had been having a normal sex life. Mrs. X was indignant and said, 'Sir, I'll have you know that the X's are Christians. When my children were born, I stopped sleeping with my husband (meaning they stopped having sexual intercourse) and have not slept with him since. When my daughter's third child was born, I instructed her to stop sleeping with her husband. She has not slept with him in five years. Sir, I'll have you know that all this talk about sex is beneath the dignity of the Christian life.' The couple divorced.

"Any enlightened person knows that the ideas of Mrs. X were perverted and unchristian. To hold Christianity responsible for Mrs. X's ideas is like holding medical science responsible for the many naive beliefs people have about the cause and cure of diseases.'"[9]

I had been invited to speak to a Human Sexuality class while lecturing at a university in the southwest. Just before I was introduced, I borrowed the class textbook from one of the students. As I started to page through it, I came across a statement the student had underlined. I couldn't believe what I read: "Anyone who has religious convictions will probably experience a deteriorated sex life." Despite volumes of scientific evidence to the contrary, these secular writers are still expounding this myth.

Experiencing My Point

By now you may be saying, "Hold it. Don't drown me in statistics. I'm living in the real world of getting along with my husband."

Let me share some personal insights to balance the many statistics I have quoted. In a marriage relationship, the husband and the wife draw closer to each other as they draw closer to Christ. Let me illustrate with an equilateral triangle. The husband and wife are the two bottom corners and Christ is at the top. If the two bottom corners want to move closer together, they have to move closer to the top corner. (For a further understanding of this I would suggest you read *I Married You* by Walter Trobisch.) My personal relationship with God through Jesus Christ has helped to make me a better lover, a better husband and a better friend to Dottie.

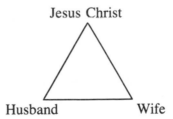

Jesus Christ

Husband   Wife

Years ago, well before I met Dottie, I started looking for answers to some of life's most perplexing questions. Since a lot of people "had religion" where I was raised, I thought that perhaps religion was the answer, so I took off on religion. I was involved in religion morning, afternoon and evening. I must have gone to the wrong church, though, because I actually felt worse than when I started.

Next I thought, "Well, maybe education is the answer." As a farm boy I knew that the cream rises to the top. It must be the educated people who have inner joy, happiness, meaning and even the power to be free. With this in mind, I enrolled in the university. What a disappointment to someone trying to find truth and purpose in life!

The first university I went to was in Michigan, and I was probably the most unpopular student on campus with the professors. I wanted answers. I used to buttonhole them in their offices. I think some of them would turn off the lights and pull the shades when they saw me coming. It didn't take me long to realize that a lot of those faculty members and students had more problems, less meaning to life, and more frustration than even I had. In fact, my economic theory professor could tell me how to make a better living, but he couldn't tell me how to live better.

Then I thought, "Maybe prestige is the answer. Find a 'calling' and give your life to it." Those at my school who seemed to hold the purse strings and carry a lot of weight were the student leaders, so I ran for various political offices and got elected.

It was neat knowing everyone on campus, making decisions, spending the money of others to achieve the ends I wanted. I enjoyed it. But every Monday morning I woke up the same person. I usually had a headache because of the night before, and I always had the same attitude, "Well, here we go again for another five days." I sort of endured Monday through Friday; my happiness revolved around Friday, Saturday and Sunday nights. The whole vicious cycle would start again the following Monday.

Eventually I became frustrated. I doubt if too many students in the universities of our country have been more sincere in trying to find meaning and truth and power and purpose in life than I was, yet I hadn't found it.

Hope Springs Eternal

About that time I noticed a group of people around campus. There weren't very many of them, only eight students and two faculty, but there was something markedly different about their lives. They seemed to know where they were going in life, and that was very unusual. A lot of people in our society are like a fellow I saw at the University of Chicago. He was walking around (it was probably registration week) with a large sign on his back saying, "Don't follow me. I'm lost."

These people not only seemed to have direction, they seemed to have convictions. I don't know about you, but I enjoy being around people who have convictions, even if they don't agree with me. Some of my closest friends are opposed to some things I believe. I admire people who not only know why they believe what they believe, they also know why they don't believe what they don't believe. That's just as important, and this group of people seemed to know all of that.

Furthermore, these people reflected a unique kind of love in the way they treated people. I had observed that while most people talked a lot about love, these people *demonstrated* something special in their relationships with others. They had something I didn't have and I wanted it, so I made friends with them.

Several weeks later, we were sitting around a table in the student union. I recall that six of the students were there, along with two of the faculty—one of them with his wife. The conversation started to turn to God. Let's face it: If you are insecure, whether you are a student, a professor, a business person, a waitress or anything else, you have to put on a big front when the conversation gets to God. Every university, every high school, every office and every lunchroom has a hot shot—the person who says, "Christianity? That's for weaklings, not for people with brains."

Do you know what I've found to be true? Invariably, the bigger the front an individual puts up, the greater his or her emptiness on the inside. That's the kind of front I was putting on. Their conversation irritated me. I wanted what they had, but I didn't want them to know, although the whole time they knew I wanted what they had and also that I didn't want them to know I wanted it. (You can see the dilemma I was in.)

I leaned back on my chair and tried to act nonchalant. I looked over at this one young woman. (She was *good looking!* I used to think that all Christians were ugly. I figured if you were a loser and couldn't make it anywhere else, you became a Christian.) I said, "Why are you so different from the other students on campus?" She looked back at me with a little smile, which can also be irritating if you're in the wrong mood, and said two words I never thought I'd hear in the university as part of the "solution." She said, "Jesus Christ." "Oh, come on," I said, "I'm fed up with religion, the church, and the Bible. Don't give me that garbage about religion." She must have had a lot of courage and strong convictions because she looked me in the eye, and this time she didn't smile. "Look," she shot back, "I didn't tell you *religion*; I told you Jesus Christ." Well, I apologized to her because I'd been very rude. I hadn't been brought up to be rude. I said, "Please forgive me for my attitude, but to tell you the truth, I'm sick and tired of that kind of thing. I just don't want anything to do with it."

I couldn't believe what happened next. Right there in the university, these students and faculty challenged me to intellectually examine who Jesus Christ was. I thought it was a joke! They went into detail about God taking on human flesh in Jesus Christ, His death on the cross for the sins of humanity, His burial, His literal resurrection on the third day, and then they had the nerve to insist on His ability to change a person's life in the twentieth century.

A Surprise Ending

How ridiculous! It was my opinion that most Christians had two brains, one was lost and the other was out looking for it. I used to wait for a Christian student to speak up in class so I could tear him up one side and down the other. I usually beat the professor to the punch. I knew answers to any argument a Christian could bring up, but these people kept challenging me over and over again, so I accepted their challenge.

I have to admit I did this with the wrong motivation. I did it out of pride, not to prove anything, but to refute them. In fact, the original purpose of my first book, *Evidence That Demands A Verdict*, was to write a book that would make an intellectual joke of their beliefs.

I set out to show the absurdity of Christianity, but after two years of research and a lot of money it backfired on me. I came to the conclusion that Christ had to be who He claimed to be. Faith had nothing to do with my conclusion; it was strictly intellectual. I had determined that if I could show that either of two basic areas was not true or historically trustworthy, I had won my case against Christianity.

The first area was to show that the New Testament is not historically reliable. I figured there was no question about that. It was written years later, I thought, and countless myths and legends had crept in, along with other errors and discrepancies. That's all I had to prove. It backfired!

The second area was the resurrection, which I felt would be even simpler to discount. Everything that Jesus Christ taught, lived, and died for was based on His literal resurrection from the grave, and my simple task was to show that the resurrection never took place. I thought that would be easy—I'd never met anyone who'd been resurrected. It backfired, too. In fact, the evidence was so overwhelming it provided the material for another book, *The Resurrection Factor*.

The Irresistible Force

I really had a problem. My intellect was convinced, but I still struggled. I found out that becoming a Christian (I prefer to say "a believer") is rather ego-shattering. I prided myself on my self-sufficiency. Jesus Christ challenged me to trust Him as Savior and Lord. Jesus challenged my will asking me to trust Him with my life, since He had died on the cross for my sins. To paraphrase His invitation: "Look! I have been standing at the door and I am constantly knocking. If anyone hears me calling him and opens the door, I will come in" (Revelation 3:20). I had to recognize that "as many as received Him, to them He gave the right to become children of God, even to those who believed in His name" (John 1:12).

I didn't care if He did walk on water or turn water into wine, I didn't want a "party pooper" invading my life. I couldn't think of a faster way to ruin a good time, destroy my intellectual pursuits, or impede scholarly acceptability with my peers than to let Jesus come in. My mind told me that Christianity was true, but my will said, "Don't admit it." To put it mildly, I was troubled.

Every time I was around those enthusiastic Christians, the conflict would intensify. If you've ever been around happy people when you're miserable, you understand how they can bug you. They would be so happy and I would feel so miserable I would literally get up and run right out of the student union. I became so disturbed I'd go to bed at ten at night and not fall asleep until four in the morning. I knew I had to get Jesus out of my head or go out of my mind!

On December 19, 1959, at 8:30 p.m., during my second year at the university, I became a Christian. Someone later asked me, "How do you know?" I said, "Look, I was there." That night I prayed. My prayer had four steps as I sought to establish a relationship with God—a personal relationship with His Son, the resurrected, living Christ. Over a period of time that relationship has transformed my life.

First, I prayed, "Lord Jesus, thank You for dying on the cross for me." Second, I said, "I confess those things in my life that aren't pleasing to You and ask You to forgive me and cleanse me." (The Bible says, "Though your sins are as scarlet, they will be as white as snow.") Third, I said, "Right now, in the best way I know how, I open the door of my heart and life and trust You as my Savior and Lord. Take control of my life. Change me from the inside out. Make me the type of person You created me to be."

The last thing I prayed was "Thank You for coming into my life by faith." The Holy Spirit activated my faith, which was based on God's Word and supported by evidence and the facts of history.

Now I'm sure you've heard religious people talk about their "bolt of lightning" experience. After I prayed nothing unusual happened. Nothing. In fact, after I made that decision, I felt worse. I felt sick to my stomach. "Oh no, McDowell, what'd you get sucked into now?" I wondered. I really felt I'd gone off the deep end, and some of my friends agreed. I may have felt unsure about my decision right then, but after several months I knew I hadn't gone off the deep end. My life was changed.

Changing For Good

One area I saw changed was my restlessness. I was a person who always had to be occupied; I had to be over at my girlfriend's place or somewhere in a discussion. I'd walk across campus, my mind a whirlwind of conflicts. I'd sit down and try to study or think and I couldn't. But a few months after I made that decision to trust Christ, I began to notice a kind of mental peace.

I don't mean I didn't have conflict. What I found in this relationship with Jesus wasn't so much the absence of conflict as it was the ability to cope with it. I wouldn't trade that for anything in the world, for I have come to experience in a very real way what Christ promised when He said, "Peace I leave with you; My peace I give to you; not as the world gives, do I give to you. Let not your heart be troubled..." (John 14:27).

Another area that started to change was my bad temper. I used to blow my stack if somebody just looked at me wrong. I still have the scars from almost killing a man my first year in the university. My temper was such an integral part of me that I didn't consciously seek to change it. One day after my decision to put my faith in Christ, I arrived at a crisis, only to find that my temper was gone! I have only lost control of my temper once since December of 1959. Jesus Christ changes lives.

A third area in my life which felt the transforming power of Christ was my relationship with my father. The seething hatred I felt toward him—the town drunk who abused and embarrassed our family—was changed into love and acceptance. The change was so obvious that even my father saw it, and he asked Jesus into his life.

The Bible says that if you are in Christ, you are a new creation, and I saw my father recreated before my eyes. He never drank again. I've come to one conclusion: A relationship with Jesus Christ changes lives. You can ignorantly laugh at Christianity, you can mock and ridicule it, but it works. If you trust Christ, start watching your attitudes and actions, because Jesus Christ is in the business of changing lives, forgiving sin, and removing guilt. If that doesn't improve a marriage relationship, nothing will.

What's Your Conclusion?

I've shared how I personally responded to the claims of Christ. You, too, need to ask the logical question, "What difference does all this evidence make to me? What difference does it make whether or not I believe Christ rose again and died on the cross for my sins?" The best answer is something Jesus said to a man named Thomas, the doubter. He told him, "I am the way, and the truth, and the life, no one comes to the Father, but through Me" (John 14:6).

You can trust God right now by faith through prayer. Prayer is talking with God. God knows your heart and is not as much concerned with your words as He is with the attitude of your heart. If you have never trusted Christ to forgive your sin and give you eternal life, you can do that right now. You can pray something like this: "Lord Jesus, I need You. Thank You for dying on the cross for my sins. I open the door of my life and trust You as my Savior. Thank You for forgiving my sin and giving me eternal life. Make me the kind of person You want me to be. Thank You that I can trust You."

After trusting Christ as Savior and Lord, the practical implications of biblical teachings and the need of the spiritual dimension in a relationship become quite obvious. My relationship with God affects every area of my life. It certainly makes a difference in my marriage.

Positives and Negatives in Marriage

While lecturing on the Christian perspective of love, sex, and marriage in a psychology class at a northeastern university, I was asked by a student, "What are some factors that help to produce a good marriage?" After listing both the negative and positive factors, I asked the class where they thought I had come up with the list. Most replied a book on marriage, or a psychology or sociology textbook. You should have seen their response when I pointed out that these are positive and negative factors of an intimate relationship as depicted in the Bible. Some just shook their heads in disbelief. For the first time many of these students began to consider the Bible as relevant to love, marriage and sex.

These are the positive and negative marital attributes I outlined to the class:

POSITIVE	NEGATIVE
Patience: James 1:2-4; Hebrews 10:16; 1 Corinthians 13:4; Colossians 3:12, 13	Impatience
Seeking the good of others: 1 Corinthians 13:5; Philippians 2:4; Galatians 6:2	Seeking one's own good
Giving: Luke 6:38; 1 John 4:10	Taking
Selflessness: Philippians 2:3-8	Selfishness
Truthfulness: Colossians 3:9; Zechariah 8:16; 1 Corinthians 13:6; Ephesians 4:25	Lying
Humility: Philippians 2:3-8; Proverbs 16:18; James 4:6; Colossians 3:12	Pride
Kindness: 1 Corinthians 13:3; Matthew 5:21, 22; Colossians 3:12; Galatians 5:22	Hatred
Trust: Proverbs 27:4;	Distrust

1 Corinthians 13:4, 7	Jealousy
Realistic view of self: 1 Corinthians 4:6-7, 8:1, and 13:4; Colossians 2:18; Galatians 6:4	Arrogance Conceit
Responsible: Luke 16:10-12	Irresponsible
Protective: 1 Corinthians 13:5, 6	Thinks of own reputation
Forgiving: Colossians 3:13; Matthew 11:25, 6:14	Unforgiving
Self-examining: Matthew 7:1,2; John 8:9; Luke 6:37	Judgmental
Content: Jude 15:18, Hebrews 13:5	Complains
Gratitude: Proverbs 19:3; 1 Thessalonians 5:8; Romans 1:21; Ephesians 5:20	Ingratitude
Self-Control/Even Tempered: Proverbs 16:32; Romans 5:3,4; 1 Corinthians 13:5; Galatians 5:23	Self-indulgent Temper uncontrolled
Diligent: James 4:17; Colossians 3:23	Complacent
Confidentiality: 1 Corinthians 13:7; 1 Peter 2:9; 1 Timothy 5:13;	Gossip
Gentleness: Galatians 5:23; Colossians 3:12	Harshness
Compassionate: Colossians 3:12; Luke 6:28; Galatians 6:2	Incompassionate
Sensitive/Courteous/Polite: 1 Corinthians 13:5	Rude
Faithful: Galatians 5:22	Unfaithful

You might be as overwhelmed as I was at first with the above list. You may be ready to throw in the towel before you even start, since it seems you would have to be God or some spiritual giant to experience all of the positive factors listed. Yet common sense dictates that these are plus factors in developing close, intimate relationships. Since you know you cannot produce them yourself, you may well feel frustrated.

Relax, there is good news! You spell relief H-O-L-Y S-P-I-R-I-T. Not only did God give us a high standard to live by but also gave us the strength by which to live it. The above positive factors are simply manifestations or qualities that are true of God Himself in His basic nature. In other words, God Himself is not only our standard to live by, His character is also the very essence of what should be incorporated into our lives in a love, marriage and sex union.

Our loving heavenly Father shows us His nature, who He is, in the Bible. Through the Holy Spirit He places Himself within a believer to live His life out through him. In the person of the Holy Spirit God has given us all we need to live the Christian life. The indwelling presence of God through the Holy Spirit is the source that empowers us to be the "right person" in the marriage relationship.

Accept No Subsititutes

Because of the extreme importance of the indwelling presence of the Holy Spirit I would like to repeat here what I shared in my book *His Image... My Image* on "a new sense of competence":

"The most effective way to grasp the potential competence you have through the Holy Spirit is to understand the resources available to every Christian as a result of the Spirit's indwelling presence.

"Something wonderful happened to the Lord's disciples on the day of Pentecost. They were filled with the Holy Spirit and went forth in His power to change the course of history. That same Holy Spirit who empowered the disciples to live holy lives and to be powerful and fruitful witnesses wants to work in us today. The amazing fact that Jesus Christ lives in us and expresses His love through us is one of the most important truths in the Word of God.

"Trying to live the impossible standards of the Christian life in our own strength—and failing, as we inevitably do—is bound to weaken our sense of competence. In fact, the Christian who tries to be as much like Christ as possible (a supernatural ideal) can have a worse sense of competence than the person who is not a Christian and who chooses to live by some human ideal. The standards of the Christian life are too high for us to achieve on our own. According to the Word of God, only one person has been able to succeed in keeping them—Jesus Christ. The Christian life was meant to be lived only in the power of His Holy Spirit.

"Not only does the Holy Spirit enable the Christian to be born into God's family, but the Spirit assists the Christian in spiritual growth, in producing the fruit of the Spirit.

"It is the Holy Spirit who empowers us to be fruitful witnesses. When Jesus said that we were to be his 'witnesses both in Jerusalem, and in all Judea and Samaria even to the remotest part of the earth,' He preceded this with the statement that 'You shall receive power when the Holy Spirit comes upon you.' It's not only impossible to become a Christian apart from the Holy Spirit, it's also impossible to produce the fruit of the Spirit in our lives and to introduce others to Jesus.

"From the point that we receive Christ and are indwelt by the Spirit, everything we need to be men and women of God and to be fruitful for Christ is available to us. The key lies in allowing the Holy Spirit to fill or empower our lives, so we can experience all that is available to us. It's important to realize that the word for *fill* does not mean something from without coming in but rather something already within doing the filling. That is why I prefer using the words *permeate* or *empower*.

"We are filled with the Spirit by faith, faith in an all-powerful God who loves us. When you take a check to the bank and you know you have money there, you don't go in with doubts about whether or not the bank will cash your check. You don't expect to have to beg the teller to give you the money. Instead, you simply go in faith, place the check on the counter and expect to receive the money that is already yours. In asking God to fill us completely with the Holy Spirit who is already in our lives, we again simply ask for something that is already ours as children of God.

"While you can expect to receive both your money from the bank and the filling of the Holy Spirit from God by faith alone, nevertheless you must recognize the factors that precede receiving both of these. You receive your money from the bank only when you go there with a check or withdrawal slip that is properly filled out and signed. If you go there brashly, without following the bank's procedures for disbursing funds, it's not likely that you will receive your money. Merely standing on the curb outside the bank and yelling, 'I want my money!' won't get the desired results.

Getting Ready

"Similarly, several things prepare you for the filling of the Holy Spirit. First, you must hunger and thirst for God and sincerely desire to be filled with His Spirit. Jesus' promise was 'Blessed are those who hunger and thirst for righteousness, for they shall be satisfied.'

"Second, you must be willing to surrender the direction and control of your life to Christ. As Paul said, 'And so, dear brothers, I plead with you to give your bodies to God. Let them be a living sacrifice, holy—the kind He can accept. When you think of what He has done for you, is this too much to ask?' (Romans 12:1, TLB).

"Third, confess every known sin the Holy Spirit brings to your mind and accept the cleansing and forgiveness that God promises. 'But if we confess our sins to Him, He can be depended upon to forgive us and to cleanse us from every wrong. And it is perfectly proper for God to do this for us because Christ died to wash away our sins' (1 John 1:9, TLB).

"Being filled with the Spirit is not an optional lifestyle for the Christian. God commands us to be filled with His Spirit. 'Do not get drunk on wine, which leads to debauchery. Instead, be filled with the Spirit' (Ephesians 5:18, NIV). But God does not command without providing us a way to obey His commands. He gives us the promise 'that if we ask anything according to His will, He hears us. And if we know that He hears us—whatever we ask—we know that we have what we asked of Him.'

"Christians already have the Holy Spirit dwelling within them, so they need not ask Him to come into their lives. They need only ask Him to fill and take control of every part, every hidden corner and crevice.

"While Christians are *indwelt* only once by the Spirit (at the time Christ came into our lives through the Holy Spirit), we will be *filled* with the Spirit many times. In fact, the Greek wording means 'be ye being filled,' referring to a constant and continual filling of the Spirit to control and empower one's life.

"The frustration of self-effort is eliminated when we live in the power of the Holy Spirit. He alone can give us the ability to live the holy and meaningful life we so desire.

"If you know that you desire a life filled with the Spirit, you need only to ask the Father for it. Acknowledge that you have been in control of your life, which is sin against God, the rightful ruler of your life. Thank Him for forgiving your sins through Christ's death on the cross for you. Invite Christ to take over the control of your life and the Holy Spirit to fill you with His power so that you can glorify Christ in all you do.

"As an act of faith, then thank Him for doing what you have asked. Thanking Him is not presumption, it is acting in faith that He is keeping His promises to give us whatever we ask within His will. And since He commands us to be filled with His Spirit, it is His will for all Christians to live this supernatural lifestyle.

God's Strength or Yours?

"From the sense of competence that his experience with the Holy Spirit gave Paul, he could say, 'I can do everything through Him who gives me strength.' Paul saw his adequacy not in himself but in God, whom He had come to know as an integral part of His life. 'Not that we are competent to claim anything for ourselves but our competence comes from God.'

"In studying the people whom God uses, you often find that when they yield themselves to God, He takes their limitations and turns them into strengths.

"So often people say, 'Oh, John or Mary ought to be in a special kind of Christian work. He or she is so talented, so persuasive, so gifted in that particular area.' But sometimes strengths can end up being limitations. The strengths we relied on before God had complete control of our life can sometimes become disadvantages. We tend to lean on whatever strengths were evident in us before we consciously allowed the Holy Spirit to build other strengths into our life. The strengths we had before the Holy Spirit took control are sometimes temptations for attitudes of self-sufficiency, self-centeredness and pride.

"On the other hand, weaknesses we were aware of and knew we would have to rely on God to overcome can keep us dependent on the Holy Spirit to change. These may turn into some of our greatest strengths.

"A proper perspective of yourself is understanding who you are with your strengths and good points, your shortcomings and faults, remembering that those surface strengths can become temptations for pride. Having a healthy self-image doesn't mean you don't have limitations. If you know who you are in Christ, you are free to accept your weaknesses, faults and mistakes—and not be threatened by them. Patiently and with hope, you can work through those problems without putting yourself down because you don't meet some imagined standard of perfection.

"Someone with a sturdy pillar of competence can affirm the axiom mentioned earlier, 'I'm not what I ought (or was created) to be, but I'm not what I used to be, and, by God's grace, I'm not what I'm going to be.' We can be 'confident of this, that he who began a good work in [us] will carry it on to completion until the day of Christ Jesus.'"[10]

You're wrong if you think living the Christian life is difficult. "Impossible" would be a better description if you try to live it on your own. Only the Holy Spirit can live His presence through you. God wants to be the source for making *His* character traits a reality in *your* life. The apostle Paul, noting the characteristics of an individual led by the Spirit, writes, "But the fruit of the Spirit is love, joy, peace, patience, kindness, goodness, faithfulness, gentleness, self-control; against such things there is no law" (Galatians 5:22,23). Being the "right person" from a biblical perspective is when God by the Holy Spirit lives His life and character in and through you.

Let me emphasize again that the single most important aspect of my marriage with Dottie is my personal relationship with Jesus Christ.

There not only needs to be a genuine commitment to Christ but also the desire to grow and become spiritually mature. So often a frustrated husband or wife will say about a spouse's coldness or indifference to spiritual things, "Well, I thought she (or he) would change after we were married."

Let me conclude by offering you four excellent guidelines against which you can evaulate whether or not a maturing process is taking place spiritually. These are set forth by Dr. J. Allen Petersen in his excellent book, *Before You Marry*. He points out that a couple ought to be continually growing in the following areas. You will be "the right person" if you consistently will place your emphasis here:

1. Putting priority on daily time alone with God.
2. Talking freely to others about Christ.
3. Being sensitive to sin in your life and dealing with it.
4. Increasing in obedience to the Word of God."[11]

Questions to Ponder

- Why does spiritual intimacy enhance sexual intimacy?
- Study the verses which accompany the positive marital attributes.
- What is the role of the Holy Spirit in our lives?

CHAPTER 12

THE STRESS FACTOR

Experiencing stress? Is it affecting your love life? You are not alone!

While speaking in the United States recently, the Director of the National Institute of Mental Health of England made the following statement, "The whole Western world is under stress. It is one of the fastest growing diseases in the world." Stress is a prime source of marital and interpersonal relational problems in general. It touches every one of us, and our capacity to cope with it will affect our ability daily to be the right person in a relationship.

Out of the 15,000 people surveyed in 1978 and 1979 by General Mills in a study entitled "Family Health In an Era Of Stress," 82 percent were rated as having a desperate need to learn to cope with stress. Based on studies done over the last ten years, the American Academy of Family Practitioners estimates that two-thirds of all patients seen by general practitioners have problems that are stress related.

These and similar statistics have caused many company presidents and industry leaders to be concerned. They are worried because this past year, absenteeism, company medical costs due to stress-related illnesses and lost productivity have cost their companies fifty billion dollars. And they believe that within two years, that stress cost factor will grow to seventy-five billion dollars—an average of $750 for every single worker in the United States. Families and marriages are one of the greatest areas impacted by stress. It is a prime source of marital and interpersonal relational problems in general.

Don Osgood, a management trainer with the IBM Corporation, has some excellent material concerning stress and its causes and remedies. The following article, which I am going to quote in entirety because of its excellent content and value, provides some answers to questions on stress.

117

Cause and Effect

"Have you noticed how stressed you feel when you have done something wrong and you are afraid someone is about to find out? This kind of stress is something we all contend with, because we've all done something wrong, whether it's secretly eating cookies in the pantry or breaking a law and finding a policeman around the very next corner. But there are other causes.

"Sometimes you catch stress the way you catch a common cold, by day-to-day exposure. And nobody gets alarmed because everybody knows a little stress won't harm you. Some is actually good for you. But one day you find you have been gripped by the disease of over-stress without even knowing when it started. Then you must look for a way out of your illness—for rest from a struggle that is quietly wearing you away. In this personal struggle with stress, God can give you healing when you abandon your own way.

"Relationships are one of the key factors in handling stress. When we do something wrong, or something that could hurt someone if he or she found out, we add to our stress. One of the reasons is our fear of losing our relationships. Two doctors, Holmes and Rahe, at the University of Washington Medical School, came up with forty-three life events that make up a stress scale. Of the forty-three life events, ten produce the greatest stress. Seven of these ten events are directly related to a loss of relationships, such as divorce, death of spouse, marital separation or retirement. But there is one the scale overlooks; an obedient relationship with God, who won't be pushed, coaxed or manipulated into something that is wrong for us.

"In the fourth chapter of the letter to the Hebrews, an obedient relationship as a way out of the disease of stress is emphasized, so simply that we might easily overlook it…'he that is entered into his rest, he also hath ceased from his own works….' This notion of ceasing from personal works was both a message to the Israelites concerning the Sabbath and a reference to the Promised Land. But it is also a God-given prescription for obtaining day-to-day healing from our own stress-struggle.

The Roots of Dis-ease

"The first step is one of reexamining our egos. Dr. Harry Levinson, the noted psychologist, talks about something called an ego ideal—a bright, shiny notion we have of who we might ultimately become. We'll do almost anything to see how big or how good we are, because we want to be able to like ourselves. But there is often a gap between what we are and what we'd like to be, and this gap can cause stress dis-ease—or I'll call it ego stress—because our egos are what cause the underlying problem. That's why, even though you may have been a committed Christian, you need to reexamine your way of life.

"My own experience with this kind of stress taught me a powerful lesson. I was asked by my company if I would consider an assignment in Japan. It was a great ego builder, but I knew that I might create family problems if I accepted. I had already moved my family to four different cities and after one of these moves my oldest son, then fifteen, ran away for several days. I should have known that I had no business considering another such move now that another son had reached the critical age of fifteen. But I let management consider me along with others for six long weeks. 'I won't try to sell myself, God. I'll just let them decide.' My wife, Joan, said, 'I'm praying for direction for us, Don.' And I knew the way she said it that she didn't want to go. My fifteen-year-old son said flatly, 'I don't want to go, Dad!'

"At the end of the sixth week the announcement was made that another person was selected. 'It's all right,' I said. But it was just two days later that I developed an intestinal disorder that wouldn't go away, and only then did I begin to realize how deep the struggle had been. After four days of discomfort I was awakened in the middle of the night by the same trouble, and with the honesty that exhaustion brings, I prayed softly, 'I understand now how deeply I have struggled, Lord. Heal me of my sin of preoccupation with my wants. Heal my relationship with my family...and, please, heal me of my physical discomfort, too.'

"I never had to get out of bed that night because my sin was forgiven and my difficulty instantly vanished along with the tension. I had finally learned a powerful lesson. A person can get so busy gaining a place in life that he risks losing his own family and spiritual relationships. And along the way we bury down deep our knowledge of what's right.

A Deadly Preoccupation

"If your way is to take charge of life without also learning to really let go, or if you are conducting an ego struggle with God, then you are living in your kingdom instead of His way.

"The ability to take charge is an important skill in our busy world, and ego is an important part of that. God created us with egos to enable us to achieve. But it's the preoccupation with ourselves that God objects to, because that is what keeps us in bondage to ourselves. Probably ninety percent of our life is spent in thinking about ourselves and in racing after our ego ideal. But His plan for us when we are overstressed is that we cease from our own works and become occupied again with Him. According to an old Spanish proverb, 'It is not the burden but the overburden that kills the beast.' In other words, it's the normal stress of the day plus the worry over ourselves that harms us. Jesus knew this when he said, 'Come unto me, all ye that labor and are heavy laden (overburdened, overstressed, exhausted from the rat race) and I will give you rest' (Matthew 11:28). It is a way of restful obedience.

"But there is another kind of stress caused by the turmoil of indecision. When I was living in Kansas City, trying to decide which way to turn because of a company reorganization, I was offered a job in Chicago and another in New York. I wanted to stay in Kansas City, but Joan didn't. I thought I was being called into a ministry there with an evangelical organization, but they said, 'Both you and your wife must feel the call,' and Joan just didn't feel it. After several weeks of unrest, I consulted a Christian brother who suggested a way to resolve the stress of uncertainty when there is disagreement among the people who are most deeply involved.

"'There are three things you must do,' he said. 'Confess all the sin in your life and clear away anything that stands in the way of a pure relationship with God. Next, explain your problem to Him as frankly as you can. Last, believe that He is now working out your answer—not that He will, but just that He is. Then let it go.' That's called abandonment. I had taken the first two steps, but not this third and most important one. When I told God I believed He was working out the answer—in that moment—I found out where I was to go just minutes later.

"A businessman was late for a speaking engagement in Rochester, Minnesota, and was just leaving Minneapolis, eighty miles away, with no lunch and only an hour and a half before he was to speak. Though he normally drove at fifty-five miles per hour, he sped down the highway at a breathtaking eighty-five, until a state trooper spotted him. He saw the trooper looking right at him as he raced by, and he prayed, 'Lord, you know I need to get to Rochester. Don't let him stop me.' But something checked him and he added, 'If that's all right with you.' Apparently it wasn't all right, because the trooper stopped him and asked where he was going. He said, 'To give a lecture on stress.' Then, feeling very sheepish, he added, 'And I feel very stressed right now.'

"We don't want to meet people when we've been doing wrong, especially people in authority. But it reduces stress to admit we're wrong. Though it's not fun, it's strangely more freeing to be caught when we're guilty than to carry around the knowledge of guilt. Sooner or later we must come to terms with our guilt or lose the openness that makes a real spiritual relationship possible.

Impossible Expectations

"It works the same way with stress caused by self-doubt. A Ph.D. friend of mine began to feel that his company was counting too much on his ability to discover new technical solutions and that he wasn't making the progress he felt he ought to make. His nagging doubts that he couldn't live up to the expectations of others finally landed him in the hospital, until he realized that secure relationships are built on who we are, not on what people want us to be. When a psychiatrist finally asked my friend after a year of counseling, 'Why are you so hard on yourself? God loves you,' he began to be healed.

"If we are still running our lives on the assumption that God expects us to be good, we are living a lifestyle of ego stress, however unaware of it we may be. When we realize that God loves us, knowing that we can't be good without him, we are getting closer to freedom. Christ's cure is, in effect, 'Don't try harder. Don't even think harder. Instead of going your own way, yield more.' He said it a different way in the Sermon on the Mount: 'Consider the lilies.' But the more successful we become, the harder it is to see the lilies, let alone consider them. When we really consider a lily, we begin to realize that it is beautiful just by being what God wants it to be, without being fretful about what it might become or what it can't become.

"If you won't relearn how to trust in our Lord's plan, you may be flirting with an anxiety condition somewhere down the road. Christ had strong feelings about this. 'Don't be anxious,' He said. When a task is so huge that you can't see the end of it, but you know you must get it done in a month, decide exactly how much you will do today. Don't get sidetracked by what you must have accomplished two weeks from now. This is a practical way of following Christ's statement that we are not to be anxious about tomorrow.

"Instead of healing your anxiety, Christ wants to heal you of the condition that could lead you there. If you have reached the point where you can't consider the lilies, day by day, you may already be living a lifestyle of stress. Here are some of the day-to-day stress signals to be aware of:

"*An unexplained change in your effectiveness.* You suddenly realize you are unable to perform satisfactorily in an activity that you used to do well.

"*Irregular performance.* You were highly effective just last week, but this week, for some reason, you can't seem to get anything done.

"*A pattern of absence.* You find yourself taking a day off or filling up your time with other 'important' things when a certain activity or appointment with someone is coming up.

"*Cooled relationships.* People with whom you used to get along well are not as warm and natural with you as they used to be.

"These and other signals indicate that stress may be getting to you and that you should do something about it.

"What are some day-to-day causes of preoccupation with ourselves and the resulting faithlessness and disobedience we may have?

"*Sudden change.* Whether we bring it about ourselves or whether someone else does. Has life shifted you into a new responsibility that you aren't ready for, or one that calls on your weaknesses instead of your strengths? Have you just moved or are you about to move?

"Thwarted ambition. Have you become middle-aged without reaching the life goals you once hoped to achieve, and with little chance you'll ever reach them?

"The fear as you grow older that your capabilities are waning. Usually this fear is groundless. Your capabilities change as you mature, but you develop new strengths to offset reduced ability in others.

"Personality clashes. These often occur because someone is trying to bend you to their desire for your life—or you are trying to bend someone to your notion of the way they should live. Either way, people don't like to be changed by others, and when the attempt is made, stress occurs. Sometimes it should, such as during the parental guidance years. But disciplining someone in the way of the Lord and controlling or manipulating that person are two entirely different things. Disciplining should happen. Controlling should not—whether you are a minister or a manager or a mother.

"Doing something that violates your conscience. It takes maturity and courage to stand up for what you believe, to say to your neighbor or your superior, 'This is something I won't do.' It may cost you a return invitation or even a job sometime during your life, but it shows a special loyalty and it helps you to live with yourself. As a Christian you need to learn how to live with yourself without being preoccupied with self. That's not easy, but it's vital.

The Strength of Weakness

"Here are some practical, preventive maintenance steps to help keep you from anxious living—from grabbing back the style of living— from your own strength. You should consider these steps only after you have renewed an obedient relationship with God and believe He is doing His work in you. Then you can take some action.

"Learn to temporarily set aside your problems. When you're in the middle of a stressful situation, develop the ability to temporarily put it out of your mind. Concentrate on something strikingly different for a predetermined time period, after which you'll return to the problem. Say to yourself, 'It's O.K. for me not to be involved in that for the next hour because I can't handle it right now.' The advice given in Proverbs 3:5, 'Trust in the Lord and lean not unto your own understanding,' really represents a faith relationship applied to a specific problem.

"Follow an unconventional schedule. Work on your difficult tasks early in the morning when you can do them with none of the distractions that cause stress. Learn to prayerfully wait for the Lord's instructions for the day by following Christ's example of rising very early in the morning to pray.

"*Write 'memos' to God*. If you're caught in a stressful situation, scribble out a forceful note explaining your feelings in plain and strong terms. Write down exactly what disturbs you. Name specific persons and actions that bother you. Get your feelings out of your system. Just writing them down often gives you a different perspective, makes the problem more manageable and relieves the stress. Don't tell yourself you don't feel bad when you do. Be honest and tell God the truth. Admit your need and ask Him to help you release the things you have written down.

"*Change your environment*. Take twenty minutes off for vigorous jogging, followed by a shower or swim. Or have a leisurely lunch by yourself. Or when stress builds up, walk off your problem outdoors. The important thing is to change your physical environment completely. Sometimes do it more elaborately. For instance, go on a weekend trip with your wife or husband without the children and rediscover the joy and the importance of your relationship. All of these are good times to reestablish your dialogue with the Lord.

"*Find a model to follow*. Think about the humanness of Christ and why he handled far more stress than you, successfully. He could do it not only because He was God, but because He did something as a person. One of the things He did was to get away by Himself. He practiced it throughout His adult life.

"*Find a 'special' someone who can help you*. Select a person or persons whom you particularly admire; whom you can trust to be honest with you and feel you can turn to for advice on your own problems. (Not necessarily one in authority over you and not someone you expect to bail you out of trouble.) Pick someone with whom you can pray in an open way, or silently. Either way, prayer with a friend who will make you honest with yourself is a special stress reliever. Recognize while you are praying that God is interested in the real source of your concerns. That's one reason why He wants two or more of us agreeing together.

"The children of Israel failed to enter into their Promised Land because of their disobedience, lack of faith in God, and tendency to trust solely in their own remedies. That truth applies to you and me. Our modern place of rest is as available as the Promised Land was to the Israelites—without years of counseling or personal struggle. But if we put our trust only in practical cures, they will prove to be band-aids at best.

"Look closely at verses nine and ten of Hebrews, chapter 4. They offer the model of rest actually practiced by God. 'There remaineth therefore a rest to the people of God. For he that is entered into his rest, he also hath ceased from his own works, as God did from His.' That's God's pretested way out of the wilderness of overstress. He replaces stress with rest. When you believe that the teachings of His

Son Jesus are commandments to be obeyed, promises to be believed and examples to be used on a daily basis, then you are beginning to reduce the ego struggle that causes stress."[1]

Tricks of the Trade

Osgood, in an interview with the DPD Digest (the house organ of IBM), gives some suggestions on how to deal with stress on the job. This is extremely important because marital difficulties and strain are often directly related to stress experienced at work. "No one needs to deal with stress all alone, but most of us try to appear cool on the job, and we often stew about things without finding someone to confide in. In a sense, we become pressure cookers, and the feelings that simmer inside finally take their toll. We need to relearn how to be honest with ourselves and others, without hurting our established relationships.

"*Find someone who can accept you as you are—weaknesses and all.* Mature relationships are built upon such acceptance. I once did this in a performance planning discussion with my manager by saying, 'I'd like to talk about some of my weaknesses. If you will tell me yours, maybe we can work together better.' That was one of the most satisfying days I have spent in my career, and it helped later when job pressures became distressful.

"*Learn how to express honest concern without judging.* The next time a colleague says something that bothers you, try saying 'When I heard you say that, I felt disappointed,' instead of 'When you said that, you disappointed me.' This is judgement. What we are really saying in the latter case is, 'You did it to me. It's your fault.'

"*Learn to express real appreciation.* Don't hold back feelings of admiration, interest or gratitude, so long as they are honest.

"*Develop the ability to satisfy yourself.* Do something, on or off the job, that you really want to do, even if it seems foolish—and ideally, with someone you like to be with. Take that trip across country or go down the river in a houseboat. Buy something you crave, as long as it doesn't put too big a crimp in your budget. Look for ways you can do at least some of the things you have been wanting to do, without hurting your relationships.

"*Help others with their problems.* In the process, you may develop a more positive perspective on your own problems."[2]

Obviously, it would be impossible for me to impress upon you too strongly that stress should not be ignored. If it is left unresolved, it will lead to personal discouragement, broken health, emotional hurts and dissolved relationships. But, if you learn to cope with stress now, you will benefit greatly in your interpersonal relationships—especially a love, marriage and sex relationship. No matter what the cause of stress in your life might be, you can learn, as I have, to cope with it.

And actually, developing good relationships with people, especially your marriage partner, is one of the very best remedies for stress. Every one of us needs someone we can lean on and confide in during times of trouble and turmoil.

Questions to Ponder

- What is causing the greatest stress in your life?
- List stress symptoms you can recognize in your life.
- What can you do right now to begin reducing stress?

CHAPTER 13

AVOID FINANCIAL BONDAGE

What is your most recent area of disagreement with your mate? If you're normal, it probably was about the way you earned or spent money. When two people come together in a marriage the earliest area of disagreement is often the use of money—and all too frequently it remains the most contentious topic for the life of the relationship. If you want to enjoy a fulfilled love, marriage and sex relationship, the ability to handle money effectively is absolutely essential.

Nothing can trouble a relationship faster than problems associated with mismanaged finances. The reason is suggested by Jesus in Matthew 6:21, "For where your treasure is, there will your heart be also." More than any other discipline, the use of money tests the motives of a person's heart. Not surprisingly, conflict over finances is one of the major causes of divorce today.

Earlier I quoted from a *McCall's* magazine survey of 30,000 women. This revealed that, "Almost one in three women said that the lack of money was a major problem between her and her husband." In fact, "Money problems ranked far above all but one of the other problems listed—the only exception being 'poor communication.'"[1] Studies reveal that it takes longer to achieve adjustment in the area of finances than in any area except sexual adjustment.[2]

The average working American spends about 80 percent of his or her time, directly or indirectly, thinking about money. "Should I buy this? Will I get a raise? Should I make this investment? How much should I spend on clothes? Should we buy a house or rent? Can I afford to fly home for Christmas? I wonder how much Fred makes a year? Should we buy a new or a used car? How much do I give back to God?"

Choose Your Master

The reason is revealed by Jesus in Matthew 6:24, "No one can serve two masters; for either he will hate the one and love the other, or he will hold to one and despise the other. You cannot serve God and mammon [wealth]." Either you will master money, or it will master you.

Since you will bring your spending habits with you into your marriage, it is important that you develop healthy financial practices while you are single. The very use or misuse of money can be a dynamic source of friction in every home. One careless or undisciplined partner can literally devastate a marriage by his or her poor control and use of money. Undoubtedly you have had opportunity to observe this in either your own home or in another home you know well.

As Christians, our only legitimate option is to serve God, and not mammon. The apostle Paul, a veteran observer of homes and churches, wrote, "For the love of money is a root of all sorts of evil" (1 Timothy 6:10a). Now please note carefully that he wrote, "the love of money," not money itself, is the "root of all sorts of evil." Money is neutral—neither good nor bad. Our attitude toward money and what we do with it alone can be evil. How you handle money speaks volumes about your relationship with God and others.

In his book, *Your Money In Changing Times*, author Larry Burkett points out that there are more than seven hundred verses in the Bible dealing with money or possessions, and that over two-thirds of the parables of Jesus were concerned with money or possessions. Jesus knew how the hearts of men would be torn between Him and money, and He made it clear that men must not only choose between serving God and money, but they also must act responsibly with the money they may have.

Hands-on Finances

With this as our background perspective I want us to look at the importance of money from both our own perspective and from God's perspective. Let's look at personal finances on a very practical level. Much of what I want to share here comes from either my own personal experience or from insights I have gained from my dear friend, Ethan Pope, a fellow staff member in Campus Crusade for Christ who writes and speaks frequently on the subject of financial planning.

1. *Establish financial goals.* One of the reasons so many couples argue (and often fight) over money is that they have never discussed their family financial goals. Many arguments arise simply as the result of differing assumptions. The husband may feel that buying a boat is a high priority, while his wife thinks that saving for a down payment on a home is far more important.

Most financial conflicts in a marriage can be avoided if you will do two simple things:

1. Establish financial goals in a budget.
2. Have regular discussions concerning your financial goals.

In Proverbs 21:5 we read, "The plans of the diligent lead surely to advantage," and putting these simple principles into action can give you the advantage of controlling your finances rather than being controlled by them.

One reason we don't have clear financial goals for our lives is that we don't know how to write them down or to make them applicable. To overcome this, you need to apply the following five steps to developing goals: pray, write, challenge, date, and measure. Let's examine each step.

The most important aspect of setting goals is **prayer**. Ask God what He would have you do with your life and with the money He has given you. James 1:5 states, "But if any of you lacks wisdom, let him ask of God, who gives to all men generously and without reproach, and it will be given to him." So, first we must trust that God will give us wisdom when we ask it of Him.

The second important point to remember is to **put your goals on paper**. Dreams usually do not become goals or realities until they are written down. This does require walking with Him on a daily, moment-by-moment basis, for before you sit down to write out your goals, you need to be sure that everything in your life is right with God, that your heart is pure, and that no known sin remains unconfessed. If everything has been made right from your end, then God will give you the wisdom that you need. If, however, there is sin in your life and you aren't dealing with it—thereby putting you willfully out of fellowship with God—it is very possible you will be setting your own goals and not the ones God would have you set.

Next, **make your goals realistic and achievable**. For example, if a person wanted to give away a million dollars this year, but is only earning $30,000, the goal, to say the least, is very unrealistic. Certainly we don't want to limit the awesome power of God to work miracles in our lives, yet we can become discouraged when we set goals we cannot reach. We need to let God work with us where we are. When we trust the Lord to help us establish a track record of achieving goals in our lives, we will gain the confidence to set and achieve even greater goals in the future.

Determining specific dates for our goals is the fourth step. A goal without a deadline or a target date is like a football without air in it. It is virtually useless.

Along with the importance of setting dates for our goals is the fifth step, **making goals measurable**. Saying "I'm going to give away a lot of money this year" is too general. How will you know you've reached that goal at the end of the year? What is "a lot of money"? You may feel that giving 20 percent of your income is a lot, while another person may think that giving 30 percent is holding back. When you are specific in your goals, you can know whether or not you have accomplished what you set out to do.

I believe the husband really needs to take a leadership role in setting goals but the wife needs to be involved actively in the decision-making process. There must be unity, or someone will get hurt.

2. *Establish a budget.* This should be one of your first financial goals. Now, wait! I know you probably don't really want to read this part, but please don't skip over it. It is too important.

The following list explains exactly what a budget is and how it can help you. A budget:

- projects income
- projects expenses
- is a written plan of action
- should be prepared by the husband and wife together
- gives you confidence in your financial condition
- frees you
- helps you be a good steward of what God has entrusted to you
- is written in pencil, not in ink, so that it can be changed as often as needed.

Larry Burkett offers these guidelines on how to work with your budget:

1. Begin a weekly financial evaluation. Once your budget is established, review your income and spending each week. Married couples need to do this together. This involves simply looking over the budget to see how you are doing—it takes no more than ten minutes. The purpose is that it is a lot easier to make spending corrections after just one week has passed than after an entire month. Burkett points out, "Two common difficulties often arise in doing financial planning: One individual will be too legalistic, the other, too lax. Trying to correct ten years of bad financial habits in one month leads to legalism. Both husband and wife must be willing to make equal adjustments. A unilateral plan to cut someone else's spending quickly becomes a point of friction.

"Laxness usually occurs when, after the budget is planned, it is filed away and never monitored. The planning process may make some feel better, but no plan is of any value until it is implemented."[3]

2. Make "Future Purchase" and "Giving" lists. You can discuss these during your weekly budget meetings. List all of the things you need or want to buy, and the needs you want to meet in the lives of your friends or your church. Then, arrange each list according to your priorities. You will find that as you discuss your dreams, concerns, needs, hopes and the pressures you are feeling, you will open up a new channel for communication in your marriage, and you will draw closer as a couple in the give-and-take of financial planning.

If you have established financial goals and a working family budget, life will become a lot easier than it has been! I have found that most financial decisions already will be made. Your financial boundaries already will have been established. If one of you wants to buy something, such as a video cassette recorder or some new ski boots, the question to ask is simple: Is the money in the budget? Is this a priority on our list of "things to purchase"? If the answer is no, the problem is solved. You don't buy it! If this is something you really want to make a priority, then review your list at the weekly session to see where changes can be made.

When it comes to investments or unusual purchases, the Bible gives clear and helpful guidelines. "With rare exceptions," writes Burkett, "...losses of God's money could be drastically reduced by observing a few simple biblical rules:

- Pray and ask God to give you a sound mind (Proverbs 3:13).
- Husband and wife communicate together and if they positively cannot agree, they shouldn't do it (Proverbs 12:14).
- Wait before acting. Your financial vision gets much better the further away you stand (Psalm 37:7).
- Stay with what you know and avoid getting involved with areas outside your expertise (Proverbs 22:12).
- If you don't have peace—stop (Proverbs 10:22)."[4]

Remember that for a budget to work, both the husband and wife must be in agreement and be committed to working on it as a team. Making a budget work is really a matter of self-discipline. It is an act of the will. It is no accident that people who establish and stick to their budgets—flexing when necessary—have their finances in order. These people are spared the ritual of throwing their hands up in frustration at the end of the month, saying, "Where did it all go?"

3. Avoid credit. Don't live beyond your means! Many people buy things they don't need with money they don't have to impress people they don't like. Credit, like money itself, is neither good nor bad, but it becomes good or bad depending on how you use it. It can be your friend or your enemy.

These days, there are tremendous financial pressures in addition to credit cards, that can lead you into debt: low down payments, rebates, easy charge accounts and installment buying. Remember that, although nearly every form of credit is based on a projection of future income, most future income is not secured. The loss of a job, a severe injury or illness, or a change in the market will not remove your obligation to pay your bills.

Young couples are a favorite target of those wanting to extend credit, especially the credit card companies. Someone fresh out of college with a job and a spouse generally has a large shopping list—clothes, furniture, appliances, a car. With credit readily available, it becomes easy to give in to impulse buying. In a very short time you can end up with a lot of things you could really live without and an awful financial burden to shoulder. I recommend that, if at all possible, you avoid buying anything on credit during the first two years of your marriage. The last thing you need is the pressure of financial bondage.

American society says, "Get it today," and most young couples listen. They want now what it took their parents twenty years to get. Bank cards can be very useful when you're in a jam, such as to pay for a dental emergency or to get your car fixed when it breaks down out in the middle of nowhere, but credit cards can put you in bondage if you use them improperly. If you use a credit card to pay for something that is not absolutely essential, promise yourself one thing: If you cannot pay the entire bill when it comes in the mail and you are forced to pay a partial amount, you will cut the card(s) in half. Many couples charge their way to temporary happiness, only to become victims of the American nightmare.

There is no quicker way to experience financial bondage than by the immature and improper use of credit. Proverbs 22:7 says, "The rich rules over the poor, and the borrower becomes the lender's slave."

Your "Thingometer"

Our culture communicates to us the need to acquire things. I like the perspective Dr. John MacArthur, Jr., has on this possession obsession, "Mr. and Mrs. Thing are a very pleasant and successful couple. At least, that's the verdict of most people, who tend to measure success with a 'thingometer.' And when the 'thingometer' is put to work in the life of Mr. and Mrs. Thing, the result is startling.

"There he is, sitting down on a luxurious and very expensive thing, almost hidden by the large number of (other) things...things to sit on, things to sit at, things to cook on, things to eat from, all shining and new. Things, things, things.

"Things to clean with, things to wash with, things to clean, and things to wash. Things to amuse, things to give pleasure, things to watch, and things to play. Things for the long, hot summers, things for the short, cold winters. Things for the big thing in which they live, things for the garden, things for the lounge, things for the kitchen, and things for the bedroom. Things on four wheels, things on two wheels, things to put on top of the four wheels, things to pull behind the four wheels, things to add to the interior of the thing on four wheels.

"Things, things, things, and there in the middle are Mr. and Mrs. Thing, smiling, pleased with themselves, thinking of more things to add to their collection...security in a castle of things!

"Well, Mr. Thing, I've some bad news for you. What's that? You can't hear me? The things are in the way?...But then, that's the problem with things. Look at that thing standing outside your house. Whatever its value to the secondhand thingdealer, it means a lot to you. But then, an error in judgement, a temporary loss of concentration, and that thing can be a mass of mangled metal being towed off to the junkyard.

"And what about all those things in your house? Are they any more secure? Yes, time for bed. Put out the cat, but also make sure you lock the door, and don't forget the windows. Watch out! There's a thief about...

"That's the way life goes. Someday, when you die, they put only one thing in the box—you. As someone said, 'There are no pockets in shrouds.' In spite of how stupid it sounds, we are basically committed to acquiring things."[5]

Things and Happiness

Having a great number of material possessions is not the key to a great marriage relationship. If it were, poor people could never be happy! Conversely, some people will intentionally deny themselves posessions in order to be "spiritual." This is also an obsession with materialism, just in a different way. Things—money or material possessions—do not make a good marriage; people do. People striving for the inner qualities of life, such as love, joy, peace, patience, kindness, goodness, gentleness, faithfulness and self-control, are filling their lives with eternal qualities that can't rust or be stolen. You can't buy integrity or compassion, yet it is intangibles such as these that make life worth living and give us peace with ourselves.

Let your material things be icing on the cake. Rejoice in the blessings God has surrounded you with, but don't let them own you. As Jesus said, "Seek first His kingdom and His righteousness; and all these things shall be added to you" (Matthew 6:33).

4. Get your personal finances in order. Another financial goal should be to organize your financial records. You can begin by simply going over the following list with your spouse. The goal is to encourage communication and to inform your spouse about where important documents are kept.

Document/Item   Location

Budget book   _____
Balance sheet   _____
Car title(s)   _____
Birth certificates   _____
House deed/rental contract   _____

Investment listing   _____

Investment listing	_____
Stocks	_____
Bonds	_____
Savings account book	_____
Will	_____
Insurance policies	_____
Car	_____
Life	_____
Health	_____
Property	_____
Current tax information	_____
Past tax information	_____
Safe deposit box and key	(don't write answer)

Financial dealings have traditionally been the husband's domain. If this is your case, try to involve your wife in as many financial activities as possible. Have her do things like paying the bills one month, or balancing the budget book or checkbook. (All of this may be done under the husband's supervision and with his help.) If you have someone do your tax returns for you, take your wife along to the meeting so that she will feel involved, even if she doesn't understand everything at first (you had to learn it, too!). In case of your death, she should know where things are, how your finances work, and who to turn to for help. Have her go to someone who knows you and would make decisions similar to yours.

5. Establish a consistent giving plan. The most important aspect of your finances is giving; it should be your highest financial priority. Nothing tests a person's commitment to God more than money.

Without going into great detail, let me share some basic principles of giving.

Give to God first. Proverbs 3:9, "Honor the Lord from your wealth, and from the first of all your produce."

You have wealth. The media wants you to think that unless you drive a Rolls and are surrounded by luxury, you are indigent. The fact is that even the poorest American generally has more than anyone of the hungry and homeless millions in the Third World. When you honestly see the value of each item around you, you will see the wealth that is there.

Give out of the first of your fruit. In other words, give to God first as you disburse your income. Don't give God what is left over, because you will usually end up shortchanging Him. Giving first demonstrates an attitude of "God is first."

Realize that God already owns everything. You are simply managing what God has lent you. Realizing you are managing God's money adds perspective to your finances. Would you be ready for an audit?

Be faithful with what you have. Jesus said, "He who is faithful in a very little thing is faithful also in much; and he who is unrighteous in a very little thing is unrighteous also in much" (Luke 16:10). You can't hope to be righteous, while being a poor steward of the money God has given you.

As you consider giving, you should not be waiting for "your ship to come in." Rather, give out of what you have right now. God doesn't want you to save so you can give a big gift. Big numbers don't impress God—He's looking for big hearts. The Scriptures tell us of a woman who had a very big heart in God's eyes. The story in Luke 21 tells of a poor widow who put two small copper coins into the Temple treasury, which pleased the Lord more than any other gift given that day. In fact, Jesus said this widow put in more than all the wealthy who gave.

Consider the return on investment. Giving to God is the best investment you will ever make, far better than stocks, mutual funds, tax-free bonds or real estate; and the returns are everlasting. You don't even need to pay a financial planner to tell you how to give! Jesus said, "Do not lay up for yourselves treasures upon earth, where moth and rust destroy, and where thieves break in and steal. But lay up for yourselves treasures in heaven, where neither moth nor rust destroys, and thieves do not break in or steal..." (Matthew 6:19,20).

Expect a harvest. In giving, just as in everything else you do, you will reap what you sow. "Now this I say," writes the apostle Paul, "he who sows sparingly shall also reap sparingly; and he who sows bountifully shall also reap bountifully" (2 Corinthians 9:6).

Be a cheerful giver. One of the things the Bible tells us is what God likes and doesn't like, and in 2 Corinthians 9:7 we read, "Let each one do just as he has purposed in his heart, not grudgingly or under compulsion; for God loves a cheerful giver."

Give only out of love. "And if I give all my possessions to feed the poor...but do not have love, it profits me nothing" (1 Corinthians 13:3).

A friend of mine once shared this thought with me, "I find it very interesting that on every U.S. coin and bill we find the words, 'In God We Trust.' It does not say, 'In This Money We Trust'!" My friend says it is his prayer that every time anyone looks at or spends money or even writes a check, the words, "In God We Trust" will flash in that person's mind.

A mature love, marriage and sex relationship cannot function in a godly way in the day-to-day dealings of life without financial responsibility. Prayerfully seek God's will and strive to be a good steward of what He has entrusted to you. Our ultimate goal is to bring glory to God, and our ultimate trust is in Him for financial freedom, for giving hearts, for mastering materialism and for happy marriages!

Questions to Ponder

- How do you establish financial goals?
- What are some biblical guidelines regarding finances?
- What is the importance of tithing—what does the Bible say?
- What is the purpose of a budget?

FURTHER HELPFUL RESOURCES:
Larry Burkett, *What Husbands Wish Their Wives Knew About Money, (Wheaton, IL; Victor Books, 1982).*

CHAPTER 17

YOURS, MINE, AND OURS

One of the less obvious areas of conflict in the love, marriage and sex relationship is the matter of possessions. I find that engaged couples, in their attempt to concentrate on intangibles like trust, friendship and love, often overlook or brush aside this rather basic and practical aspect of their relationship. While it is vitally important that such essential intangibles be the focus of their relationship, it is also necessary that an understanding be arrived at concerning possessions.

The more issues that can be brought out into the open and discussed before marriage, the better. Understandings need to be arrived at especially in those areas which involve strong emotional attachments, likes and dislikes. I am amazed at how many people allow material possessions, such as furniture for instance, to become a thorn in the flesh of a marriage.

Dottie and I counseled a couple who had never discussed possessions before getting married. After they were married they had decided she would have a checking account in her maiden name and he would have a checking account in his name. Their conversations frequently included the phrases "this is mine" and "that is yours."

Not surprisingly, they quickly ran into a problem. She had always dreamed of having early American antiques, and he was under the impression they would have Mediterranean style furniture—he had always liked the Mediterranean furniture in his parents' home. So, without ever having discussed it, this newly-married couple went shopping together... for the first and last time. From that day on he bought Mediterranean and she bought antiques. He even decided to give her some Mediterranean pieces for Christmas, which is about like buying your wife that pool table you've always wanted.

Off Their Rocker

I was unaware of this situation when I went to their house to counsel with them one night. While there I spotted an early American rocking chair which I liked very much. The more I raved about the chair, the angrier the husband got. The issue of furniture styles had become such a destructive force in their relationship that the marriage tragically ended in divorce. The Bible admonishes a husband and wife to become one in the marriage union, but this couple never did. Their terminology and points of view never changed from "me and mine" to "us and ours."

When Dottie and I got engaged we made it a point to discuss possessions, specifically furniture. I had always wanted Spanish-style furniture, and I had already found an artist in Mexico who could handmake our furniture. There was just one catch—my wife couldn't stand that style of furniture. Her taste was for early American antiques. So we prayed about the situation together, and since we planned to spend our honeymoon in Mexico, I proposed taking her to where the furniture was made. We also decided to go to furniture auctions and antique stores to look at some early American pieces.

It didn't take me long to realize that buying antiques made a lot of sense. They are, after all, the only type of furniture which goes up in value after you buy it. And on top of all that, our first house in San Bernardino was Spanish-style, so we ended up in a Spanish style house with early American antique furniture. I think God has a great sense of humor!

Check on the words you use for "possession" when describing your interpersonal relationships or when talking about your ideal love, marriage and sex relationship. You will discover a great deal about how close you are to being the right person. The individual with the best chances for success will refer to "us," "we," and "ours" far more than "I," "me," and "mine."

How It All Adds Up

We've examined together eleven personal qualities essential to the individual who wants to shoulder the responsibility and to experience the incredible benefits and joy of being the right person in a love, marriage and sex relationship. So, let me suggest you put to yourself the obvious question: Am I the right person for marriage?

In your heart of hearts you likely know the real answer. And even if you can fool yourself, you probably won't fool many others. And the various personal qualities by which you conclude whether or not you are "right" can be your basis for determing whether your potential mate is the right person. This, in turn, will lead you to the decisive question in contemplating marriage: Are we right for each other?

The groundwork for a solid love, marriage and sex relationship must be established long before you meet the person you want to marry. And the process begins with you.

Thus far in establishing this kind of solid relationship, we have worked from your view-point—from the perspective of the individual. Next we will focus on how two people can determine if the love they are experiencing is a mature love or not. But as we continue, let me give a word of caution.

Not Perfect, But Progressing

Neither you nor your potential mate is going to be perfect, nor will you ever be. The qualities we have looked at which go into becoming the right person easily can seem overwhelming. But bear in mind that not every aspect of each of them will be present or perfectly active all the time.

If your attitude is, "Well, I've never been good with money and that's just the way I am," your marriage has a problem already. If, however, your attitude is, "I've never been good with money, but starting now I'm going to work on changing that," you're on the right track. And, of course, this perspective is applicable not only to how you handle money, but also to each of the other qualities we've looked at.

What I have shown you can help you go into a relationship with eyes wide open. And when you recognize your strengths and weaknesses in advance, you will be able to see, to work at, and to trust God to refine in you those qualities which still need improvement. That way you will be prepared so God can give you a lasting marriage relationship—one that is fully pleasing to Him.

If you are truly wise, you will e thankful when God or your spouse points out a facet of your life that needs improvement. Each personal quality you invest in, each one you can straighten out now, will only increase the richness of the dividends to be reaped in the future.

Questions to Ponder

- What words do you use when discussing possessions?
- If you are considering entering into a marriage reltionship, which of the eleven characteristics discussed are present in you?
- What areas of your life still need maturing for you to be the right person?

SECTION II

MATURE LOVE IS THE KEY

How to Know If the Love You Feel Will Last

RECOGNIZING MATURE LOVE

Every day I meet more and more people who are fearful of failing in marriage. They used to believe they knew what it was all about, but now are not so sure. They want a better answer to the question, "What does it really mean to be in love?"

If you haven't yet been confronted with the exciting and frequently baffling issue of "being in love," you probably will be. Right now, you may be in a relationship where you are asking yourself if the feeling you have for a certain man or woman is true love. You may suspect that person of some superficiality, but then again he or she may seem so very real and wonderful.

Wouldn't it be great if some clever scientist could program a "super computer" to tell us conclusively whether or not we are in love, or just how long a particular love relationship would last? Unfortunately, no such "love meter" exists to indicate the depth or quality of the love we feel. The many forces at work and the differences between people in relationships make it impossible to predict the path of love affairs on charts or with statistics.

So the problem remains. How can we test love? With all your varied feelings of love toward all sorts of people, can you know whether your feelings for a certain person are genuine? Can you know if it is "the real thing"?

Removing the Guesswork

Many will instruct you just to "follow your heart." You already may know that heeding this advice can lead to a heartbreaking situation. One emotional student was heard to exclaim, "I know I've met the right girl...I can't sleep, I can't eat, and I'm flunking all my tests!"

Sounds like a case of the flu to me.

Let me suggest you change the question you are asking. Instead of "Am I in love?" ask, "Is my love mature enough to produce a fulfilled love, marriage and sex relationship?" I prefer to evaluate love in terms of maturity because I believe we are always "in love." Puppy love is a kind of love, but it differs greatly in degree and intensity from mature love. The problem with puppy love is that if you stick with it, you'll end up leading a dog's life.

Puppy love is certainly real, and it deserves the same respect given to the other feelings people may have throughout their lives. When a child comes homes and declares, "I'm in love," he or she shouldn't be ridiculed. Adolescent feelings of love are equally genuine and wonderful. They are very real to the young person feeling them and they shouldn't be taken lightly.

Thus, again, the issue isn't whether or not you are in love. The real question remains, "Is my love mature enough to lead to a commitment and a lasting relationship?" Numerical values can't be attached to degrees of love. Feelings cannot be tightly categorized. However, I believe you can evaluate a loving relationship personally to determine whether it exhibits mature qualities. Marriage specialist Dr. Evelyn Duvall explains that "if a couple find out before marriage how flimsy the basis of their love is, they are fortunate."

The secret of loving is not only being the right person, but also experiencing the right kind of love.

In the remainder of this book I am going to discuss the characteristics of mature love. Use them as a guide to evaluate the maturity of your love. But please be careful. The qualities listed are not absolutes. They are merely given to assist you in more intelligently understanding your relationship.

Being in love is a highly subjective condition. The measure of it depends a great deal on personal preference. However, regardless of your background, education and religious upbringing, the following thirteen characteristics offer a very positive and valuable way to influence your thinking and are a helpful tool for evaluating the quality of the feelings you have toward another person.

FURTHER HELPFUL RESOURCES:
Marie Chapian, *Love and Be Loved*, (Fleming H. Revell).
W. Phillip Keller, *A Layman Looks at the Love of God*, (Bethany House Publishers).

CHAPTER 15

TOTAL-PERSON ORIENTED LOVE

Marriage must be recognized as the commitment of two people to each other as total persons. Many of us, however, base our love or marriage on an overwhelming affection for just one or two aspects of another individual.

Speaking to a group of parents recently, Sol Gordon, a psychologist and director of the Institute for Family Research and Education at Syracuse University, was asked how important sex is in a relationship. He related that according to his research, sex came in ninth out of the top ten aspects of a relationship—far behind such traits as caring or loving (first), sense of humor (second), and communication (third).

Let's consider Gordon's list of the ten most important elements in a marriage. They follow here (not in order of importance) with each point expanded by family counselor, Dr. H. Norman Wright:

1. *Laughter.* Learning how to laugh and developing a sense of humor can give balance to daily life. Look for the humor in a situation instead of letting it tear you apart.
2. *Friendships.* As a couple you have some friends whom you enjoy together, but you also have some that you enjoy by yourself. This is all right and even necessary. Your spouse will be able to meet some of your needs, but there are others who have similar interests and abilities in your hobby or sporting activity, and time spent with them in this pursuit is healthy.
3. *Involvement.* As a couple, have a sense of purpose about something outside your marriage and home. As you work on a mean-

ingful project or endeavor together, you have a shared sense of involvement. Some couples teach a Sunday school class together or serve on a committee together. In my own situation, I do a great deal of teaching at a college, in churches and in seminars across the country. I am up in front speaking and teaching. Joyce, my wife, is never in front, but she is directly involved in my ministry. She prepares all of my hundreds of overhead transparencies. She knows the content of my presentations and is just as involved as if she were the one teaching.

4. *Sex.* Sexual fulfillment is an expression of shared intimacy. In order to be fulfilling, sex needs loving with it. Too many couples become blasé in their sexual relationship so that it becomes humdrum. I have encouraged many couples to read *Solomon on Sex* by Joseph Dillow (published by Thomas Nelson) for some practical suggestions on continuing the romantic side of sexuality. Sex is a part of marriage, but for some couples it is quite overrated as the main benefit of marriage.

5. *Sharing.* This means sharing thoughts, information, jobs, projects, etc. It involves the unpleasant as well as the pleasant. As I am writing this book, we are in the process of helping a new Shelty puppy adjust to our household. She is our second Shelty, and she is a potential bride for our male. Her name is Amber, but 'Puddles' would be more fitting right now! Whenever Joyce or I walk through the kitchen area (and never in bare feet!), we look for the signs that Amber is awake and roaming about. When a puddle is sighted, whoever sees it cleans it up and scrubs that section of the floor. We don't call the other person to do it. The artificiality of the male and female role structure in the home is gradually changing, and the change allows for a greater possibility of sharing based upon ability, giftedness, and cooperation rather than upon a rigid structure.

6. *Integrity.* Being a person who is dependable and trustworthy and not compromising one's beliefs and standards is a reflection of integrity.

7. *Talk.* Conversation that is interesting and informative and contains information and emotions is an asset to a marriage. Open and honest communication that is free from fear of revealing one's own feelings or of interfering in the feelings of others is important.

8. *Love* involves caring, intimacy, trust, and commitment. Consistent large and small sensitive behaviors convey love just as the words do. Involved in love is liking the other person and desiring to be with him/her.

9. *Adaptability* involves acceptance of the other person's uniqueness. Adaptability is accepting the other person as he is, without

endeavoring to make him a Xerox copy of oneself. It means allowing the other person to do and be other than exactly what you expect.

10. *Tolerance.* Another word for this trait is acceptance. Accepting the other's quirks, occasional forgetfulness, and disagreeable moods means allowing your partner to be human just as you are. When you need to express your displeasure or concern, do it in such a way that it helps the relationship rather than hinders it.[1]

More Than A Sum of the Parts

A love relationship is many-faceted, involving the complete personalities of the two lovers—the physical, social, intellectual and spiritual aspects. Just as everyone needs to develop in each of these areas to be a healthy and complete individual, so a couple needs to develop in all of these areas together.

Jesus showed a process of growth in His life. We read in Luke 2:52 that "Jesus increased in wisdom [the mental aspect of His growth] and in stature [the physical aspect] and in favor with God [the spiritual aspect] and man [the social aspect]." He was a total person, just as you are a total person. In terms of relationships, "a person is mature enough to marry when he or she is ready to love and to be loved deeply and fully as a whole person."[2]

Immature love focuses itself on just one or two areas of an individual. If a relationship is only centered on one part of a person, chances are it is the physical. This attraction can be so powerful that it can obscure the other facets of the one being loved. Love may begin with sex appeal, yet if the two individuals wish to develop a strong and intimate relationship, they will need a rich repertoire of response and interaction as total persons.

The Sex Factor Fails

When love is based on physical attractiveness and sex appeal, it doesn't last long. Exciting as sexual attraction can be, it is such a narrow factor that it cannot support itself. Before long you realize that something is lacking. In marriages based on physical appeal, the relationship is threatened when a more attractive person comes along.

The dangers of building a relationship on sex appeal or sexual gratification are seen by Dr. Owen Morgan, director of the Center for Family Life Studies at Arizona State University, when he points out that "less than one-tenth of one percent of the average couple's time is spent in any kind of direct sex play." Morgan emphasizes that "the meaning which a husband and wife have to each other in all aspects of their living together...determines the success of a marriage."[3] It is amazing that people base marriages and relationships that they want to last on something that occupies such a tiny fraction of their time.

Strong emotional or sexual feelings may obscure the shallow depth of a relationship for a while. The problem is that powerful emotions must eventually cool off. C.S. Lewis compares this to starting a car—you have to rev the engine to get it going, but if you don't let it settle down into a solid idle, you will quickly run out of gas. Marriages based on romantic expectations are bound to be disappointing. Yet in a study of undergraduates at the University of Minnesota, psychologist Ellen Bersheid found that "more than half would want a divorce if the passion went out of their marriages."[4]

The Bible tells us that love is patient. It is entirely natural to want sex before marriage, but it is entirely loving to wait until marriage. True love can postpone gratification and instead will concentrate on loving the complete person. The person who demands sexual favors as an evidence of love expresses a selfish, demanding love. The girl who yields against her own wishes shows a childish or neurotic weakness. Incessant demanding and reluctant yielding are evidence of immature love, a love which ignores the total person.

Pope John Paul II said that "husbands who merely look on their wives with lust commit adultery in their hearts."[5] Although the remark received much criticism, I believe his intended meaning was accurate. He was saying that a complete love, marriage and sex relationship must be based on love for the whole person, not simply sex. Lust within a marriage reflects a shallow attitude toward and a low esteem for the other partner.

A Simple Test

You don't marry a body; you marry a person. Physical attraction certainly plays an important role in loving a person totally, yet for a mature love to grow, the physical attraction must not overshadow or make up for another aspect of the person. Ask yourself this question: Could we enjoy spending an evening together without any physical contact whatsoever? If you wouldn't truly enjoy it, your love isn't mature. I also like to challenge people to the "thirty day love test," to see if they make it that long without even holding hands and still enjoy each other. Most people boast at the beginning that they will have no problem doing the test, but have to face reality after a couple of days when frustration and irritation set in. So many couples have confessed to me that it was the "thirty day test" which showed them the narrow focus of their "love." They had to face the unpleasant fact that they were not in love, just physically attracted.

Monochrome Relationships

Focusing a relationship on one aspect of the individual can take many forms. Some will base their love for another on the ability to enjoy each other socially. As one divorcee shared with me, "We got along so well together and had such a fun time dating that it seemed like love." It is not unusual for a couple to think that since they enjoy each other's company so much, they must be in love. Well, you can have a hilariously good time with a chimpanzee, but that doesn't mean you should marry one! The trouble with this type of relationship is that when problems develop and frustrations set in, it takes more than having fun together to deal with them.

As I mentioned before, during my post-graduate studies I dated a young lady named Paula. We were very compatible and had fun together, but we eventually broke off our dating relationship. We realized that what we had wasn't enough to build a lasting, intimate marriage, and we had allowed our good times together to overshadow the missing areas of our relationship.

Some people get bored with their mate unless they are doing something exciting together. Mature love loves the other for what he or she is, not just for the good times you have.

Still others base their love on the spiritual side of their relationship. They rationalize that they pray together, enjoy studying the Bible together and have been used of God to lead others to Christ, so it must be love. Since they have a meaningful devotional life and the same spiritual desires and goals, they reason that they were meant for each other. In their eyes, love for Jesus equals love for each other.

Does that mean since I love Jesus and Billy Graham loves Jesus, we should get married? People who base their love on spiritual closeness overlook the fact that Jesus didn't just proclaim the gospel for the salvation of men's souls. He taught and asked questions to challenge their minds and He healed their bodies. He cared about the interpersonal relationships of others, their fears, their hopes for the future. Jesus cared about the total person. The spiritual aspect is *vitally* important, but it is no basis for a lasting marriage.

Marrying For Money

Still others base their relationship on finances. As one young man complained to his fiancée, "I thought you said there was something about me you liked." She replied, "There was, but you spent it all."

Dr. Howard Hendricks makes the acute observation that "in a proper love relationship you enrich the totality of the other person's life. In this kind of relationship a person who has been married twenty or forty years is still excited about his wife, much more so than on the first night of his honeymoon. Why? Because he didn't marry a body. If he had, that would have burned out a long, long time ago. He married a person, and every year that goes by, the person becomes enriched. Therefore, his relationship is enriched.

"Think of the poor guy who marries a girl only as a body, but after he's married to her a while, he discovers that she has a beautiful body, but she's a dunce. He can't even converse with her. Spiritually, she's an infant and could care less. Socially, she's a handicapped person. He realizes that he really got a bad bargain, no matter how attractive she may have been at the beginning. What a difference to find a person who is attractive in every area. She may not be particularly attractive to someone else, but to you she is extremely lovely."[6]

Digging For Truth

Ask yourself these questions: Do I love the way this person acts in public? How about the way he expresses himself? Could I be happy knowing that I will hold conversations with this person for the rest of my life? Do I like the way she reacts when I'm feeling down? If I were invited to a reception at the White House, would I be proud to have this person accompany me as my spouse?

The disastrous results of many marriages often come about because the relationship is not based on a total response to a total person. Without this total response, love is immature and incomplete.

We need to take care, though, to separate the person from his or her activities. My wife doesn't love me because I am a speaker and author. She helps me in what I *do*, but she loves me for who I *am*. A man shouldn't marry a woman because she is a great cook, or a woman marry a man because he provides her with important social contacts. "A marriage is a commitment of two people not to exchange products or services but to escape the psychology of exchange altogether. Each partner receives the other as a whole person, for what he is rather than for what he agrees to do."[7]

Dottie shares that the way in which we responded to each other was different from her previous dating experiences. "With Josh I was total-person oriented. I was attracted to him physically, but I was also attracted to his mind and his manners. I was challenged by his brains, the choices that he made, his spiritual depth and the way he is friendly to every person that comes within an eighty yard radius of him." This is a total response to a total person.

Knowledge of a person should be nurtured by our dating habits. We should plan dates which put us in situations that will help us get to know the other person. We need to see the quality of our communication. One of my greatest challenges was getting to know Dottie intellectually. She has a sharp mind and is probably one of my best editors.

One counselor shares that there is only one way "to guarantee a continuing area of common interest during marriage, and that is to build a relationship. How? See your friend in all sorts of different circumstances. Play Monopoly or chess with him, and see how he reacts when you beat him. You might discover that Romeo has a really hot temper. *Do I want to live with that for the rest of my life?* you ask yourself."[8]

Mature love is total-person oriented. This not only means loving and accepting another as a total person, it also means being loved and accepted for what you are in all areas. Some can give this total love, but cannot bring themselves to open up in every aspect and be wholly loved, even though they may want to. Not to be loved as a total person is to starve. Not to love another as a total person is to suffocate.

Questions to Ponder

- Why is it dangerous to build a relationship on sex appeal?
- What does it mean to have a love that is "total-person oriented?" Be specific.
- What are some of the most important elements in a marriage—and why?
- What can you do to get to know the *whole* person in a dating relationship?

C H A P T E R **16**

SPELL IT *G-I-V-E*

How do you spell love? How would you define the attitude of a person truly in love?

When people ask me to define love I reply that when you reach the point where the happiness, security and development of another person is as much of a driving force to you as your own happiness, security and development, then you have a mature love.

True love is spelled G-I-V-E. It is not based on what you can get, but rooted in what you can give to the other person.

Researchers Dr. Paul Ammons and Dr. Nick Stinnett, whom I referred to earlier, found that one of the important common denominators among people involved in good, healthy relationships is that they are giving people. Evelyn Duvall, who has helped so many in the area of love, writes, "Love that lasts involves a real and genuine concern for others as persons, for their values as they feel them, for their development and growth."[1]

Mature love is other-person centered. In his book, *Marriage Is For Love*, Dr. Richard Strauss writes that "this greatest satisfaction is in making others happy. We will never find happiness by simply looking for it. The more we look, the more frustrated and disappointed we become. Selfishly seeking our own enjoyment yields nothing but unhappiness. Unselfishly living for the good of others brings rich rewards." Strauss adds, "Mature love involves growing from a state of receiving much and giving little toward a state of cheerfully giving everything and demanding nothing in return."[2]

What Do You Want Most

The commonly held attitude, "I want what I want, when I want it" is the fundamental attitude that causes wars and international friction.

The same force that destroys nations, also destroys marriages and families. I believe we could solve a majority of the problems plaguing the world today if we could only develop an attitude of self-giving, of putting someone else's needs first. Nearly all marriage and family relationships could be healed by a simple but profound change in our attitudes.

Elof G. Nelson supervises a twelve-hour marriage preparation course each spring as part of the religion and health program at Fairview Hospital in Minneapolis. He relates this story in *Your Life Together*:

"Shortly after they had married, John began to live as he had during his single days. He loved basketball. Since the basketball season was in force, he once again joined the three teams he had played with during the past five years.

"Within two months of his wedding day, John was gone from home Monday through Friday evenings, either for practice or playing games. On Saturday afternoon, he brought several of his friends home to watch the college games on television. This was his life—fall, winter and early spring of the first and second years of their marriage. When spring came, the same type of commitments were made with a baseball team.

"Bitter quarrels grew out of this. John rarely spent an evening with Nancy. When he was home, he spent his time reading every sports magazine he could purchase. She felt he had married a housekeeper, but really had not taken a wife. Then he began going out with the boys nearly every Saturday and Sunday evening. It was obvious that he would not settle down to married living. His favorite phrase was, 'I'm not going to have anyone tamper with my way of life.' "[3]

John was obviously still thinking and living only for himself, without taking his wife's desires into consideration. He truly modeled the "I want what I want" philosophy, which clearly made for a bad marriage.

On a flight from Los Angeles to Atlanta recently, I decided to talk to the man sitting next to me. Most of the time I talk about one of the two things which are usually on my mind—Jesus Christ or my wife. I thought this time I'd start with my wife.

"Are you married?" I asked him.

The question just about brought him right up out of his seat.

"Oh, no, man, that's not for me," he said so loudly that everybody for five rows could hear.

"Oh, it isn't?" I said, and started telling him about my wife, my two daughters, my son and the relationship we have.

Fifty/Fifty Failure

Pretty soon his attitude changed, and he said, "Well, maybe some day I will get married. But let me tell you, mister, for me it's going to be fifty/fifty."

I said, "Please, don't get married!"

A maximum relationship involves giving 100 percent, no matter what the response is. The problem with a fifty/fifty relationship is that you always are trying to decide whether the other person has done his or her part. Somehow it never seems to be enough. When you give 100 percent, you are free to love and accept that other person unconditionally.

There is a wonderful reward when you make giving a priority. You will find that when you give 100 percent, you get back 150 percent. When a person knows he is loved unconditionally, he can't help but respond in kind with love. You always will get back more than you give.

When your love is mature, you will be concerned not only about having your needs met. You'll be equally intent on fulfilling those of the other person. And whenever those needs seem in conflict with yours, mature love does not have to flip a coin to decide whose needs will be taken care of first. Mature love desires to reach out to the other person first. You will find that the needs of the other person are more important to you than your own.

C.S. Lewis observed, "In one high bound, [love] has overleaped the massive wall of our selfhood; it has made appetite itself altruistic, tossed personal happiness aside as a triviality and planted the interests of another in the center of our being."[4]

Lewis goes on to compare love between two people to a violin and a bow. In the hands of a skilled musician, the two yield a beautiful sound which can hardly be imagined when viewing the bow and violin separately. Similarly, when a man and a woman come together in a mature and giving love relationship, the beauty and harmony which exists when the two are together is hard to imagine when seeing them apart.

Giving Until It Hurts

One major aspect of giving is the taking of the other person's feelings and opinions into consideration when making decisions. A young couple, Cindy and Kip, did not experience a mature love relationship even after eighteen months of engagement. Cindy failed to consider Kip's feelings and opinions when making decisions about their relationship. She took for granted that he would be enthusiastic about her plans. He finally realized that he was merely a source for Cindy to satisfy her own love needs. *She* was planning *their* relationship, and he felt like he was expected to go along quietly with each of her one-way decisions. He couldn't even give to her, because she wasn't open to take from him.

Mature love, however, is willing to sacrifice. When you truly care about the other person's happiness, security and development, you will be willing to back up your love with actions.

Our model of mature love is Jesus Christ. His love was willing to sacrifice. He was a living example of His teachings on love, "Greater love has no one than this, that one lay down his life for his friends" (John 15:13). The purpose of Jesus's life and death on the cross was not only our salvation, but also "that My joy may be in you, and that your joy may be made full" (John 15:11). In Ephesians 5:1,2, Paul emphasized our need "...to be like Him and live in love as Christ loved you, and gave Himself up on your behalf as an offering and sacrifice whose fragrance is pleasing to God" (New English Bible).

Following Christ's example, Paul said, "Let each of us make it a practice to please (make happy) his neighbor for his good and for his true welfare, to edify him and build him up spiritually" (Romans 15:2, Amplified Bible).

Your love is mature when you care more about the relationship and the other person than your own desires. It is mature when common goals and values become a priority with both of you and when winning and proving yourself right cease to be important.

Questions to Ponder

- Why doesn't the 50/50 relationship work?
- In what ways is Jesus Christ a model for love that is willing to give and sacrifice?
- In what ways is giving demonstrated in a mature relationship?

CHAPTER   # 17

SHOW RESPECT
and REVERENCE

You and I love to laugh when comedian Rodney Dangerfield complains that he gets no respect. But when respect is absent from real life relationships, it is no laughing matter. I am amazed at how many people in loving relationships fail to give their partner even the common respect they regularly show to strangers. Family counselor Judson Swihart based a helpful book on this point titled, *How to Treat Your Family As Well As You Treat Your Friends*.

A critical indicator of mature love is the level of respect and reverence you show for the loved one. In a mature relationship this reverence and respect will be mutual. If respect and reverence are not present in a relationship, love ceases to be love and becomes merely self-seeking passion.

Respect is shown by giving the other person freedom to grow and mature. Respect says, "You're O.K. and I admire you the way you are." Respect encourages the one loved to be genuinely himself or herself and to grow and develop, not for the sake of serving the spouse, but simply for his or her own sake.

Reverence is an attitude of high regard for another that contains no hint of exploitation. Mutual esteem protects the marriage from being victimized by the inevitable ups and downs it will encounter.

Author and family counselor Larry Christenson observes, "If a husband's tenderness and care for his wife depend upon the way she looks or the way he may happen to feel on any given day—if the wife's respect for her husband fluctuates with her moods, or her judgement as to how well he is satisfying her standards and expectations—that marriage is on shaky ground. Love has become the pawn of passing moods and feelings. God means for love in marriage to be built upon a more stable foundation. That foundation is a regard for the position in which the mate has been placed by God."[1]

The respect and reverence two persons have for each other preserves the integrity and individuality of both persons in a love relationship.

"Ultimately," says psychologist Nathaniel Branden, "romantic love must be defined as a passionate spiritual-emotional-sexual attachment that reflects a high regard for the value of each other's person."[2]

One of the most insightful authors on love, John Powell, writes, "We know that if the bud of a flower is injured by hostile forces, like an unseasonal frost, it will not open. So, too, a human person who is without the warm encouragement of love, and who must endure the chilling absence of praise and affection, will remain closed in on himself."[3]

The Revealing Question

A key area where lack of respect leads to manipulation is sex before marriage. Respect and reverence does not use exploitive phrases like, "If you love me, you'll let me." That deserves the response, "If you really loved me, you wouldn't persist," or, "Do you love me so little you have to have sex to prove it?"

The "everyone's doing it" plea is self-centered hedonism disguised as love. A good reply would be, "Then it shouldn't be hard to find someone else." The selfish question "Would you like to get in the back seat?" can be defused with "No, I'd rather sit up here with you." I encountered a classic line when a student once asked me, "Mr. McDowell, could you help me?" I said, "What's the problem?" She replied, "My boyfriend told me if I didn't follow through with the sex act, it would affect my kidneys."

Any of the above or similar phrases or lines reflect some of the cheap attitudes and motivations that pervade many alleged "love relationships."

At a singles' conference in Chicago a woman asked me a very sensitive question. Later, when I related her story during a lecture at UCLA, I neglected to mention that it had taken place in Chicago. After the lecture an angry graduate student approached me, thinking his girlfriend had told me about him and that I had shared it with the entire audience.

The story concerned a young lady who was pregnant and who asked my opinion on abortion. I said, "Before I give you my answer, can I ask you a personal question?" She said, "Yes," and I asked her, "Why did you enter into that intimate physical relationship with your boyfriend?" She answered, "Josh, I always wanted to wait for the right time; the right relationship, but the pressure got too great. He kept saying to me, 'Honey, if you love me, you'll let me. Darling, if you care about me, you'll let me. Oh, Joyce, if you love me, you'll let me.'"

So I asked her, "Now that you're pregnant, what is the great lover saying?"

I knew exactly what she was going to say from hundreds of phone calls, letters and counseling situations. She said, "Now he's telling me, 'Honey, if you love me, you'll get an abortion. Darling, if you care about me, you'll get an abortion.'"

Countering Cheap Shots

"If you love me, you'll let me," is one of the cheapest and most degrading statments you can make to someone in a relationship. So if a man or a woman is pressuring you to give in sexually, the first thing to say is, "No." If the person persists, share your heart and say, "Do you know how this makes me feel?" And if sharing your feelings doesn't work, tell the person, "Good-bye." It is not a relationship you would want to be involved in because you are looked upon and treated not as an individual with value, but as an object to be used.

A lot of people come to me and say, "Josh, I want to wait." Or, "I haven't waited until now, but from now on I want to wait for the right person and marriage." Then they add, "I need to know how to explain to the person I'm dating why I want to wait."

I tell them, "If you want to wait, you ought to know why. If you say no and the person persists, it is clear that this person doesn't truly love you. There is no love involved. Basically, all that person wants is sexual release and to gratify his or her desires. You have good reasons to wait, and you should not have to explain yourself."

Anyone who will push you in the area of sex is likely to push you in another area later—maybe lying, cheating, or something else. It is a character flaw the person has developed over the years, and it will surface again. Remember, the quality of one's love life is a reflection of one's character.

What Do You Expect?

In *The Total Couple*, Albert Lee and Carol Allman Lee tell the classic story of the teacher who made the mistake of linking IQ test scores to individual students.

"It seems a teacher, on the first day of class, was given a list of the children's names; each name was followed by a two- or three-digit number. At the end of the course, the children's grades coincided with the numbers the teacher had been given. The student with '140' after his name received an 'A', while the student with '87' after his name received an 'F'. Only after marking grades did the teacher find out that those original numbers were not IQ scores, but locker numbers. The teacher had made assumptions about the students' abilities, and they all lived up (or down) to those expectations. In teaming up, you ought to assume the highest score possible for your mate."[4]

In her piece, "The Secrets Behind Successful Marriages," Madora Holt writes about the importance of respect. She tells the story of a woman who felt she had been fulfilled in the relationship with her husband. "When we got married, my parents said the marriage would not last six months, and I'd always have to work to support us. They were wrong on one count. We have weathered a great many hurricanes, and I have always been the breadwinner. With my husband's patience, affectionate respect, and saving nature, I was able to turn a talent into a productive, lucrative, exciting and long career. Had he not wisely watched over and guided our investments, I might have ended up as so many of my contemporaries—with very little or penniless.

"Respect, mutual respect, is the key. Example: At one point of my career I was at the top of my profession and earning a great deal of money. A man appeared on the scene whom I thought I could look up to. He was gregarious, brilliant, fun loving, and a multi-millionaire. I separated from my husband and filed for divorce, hoping that at last I would be married to a man who was better than I. I learned from a friend that he had called her when I was out of town with the idea of 'getting better acquainted.' I knew his wife had divorced him for infidelity. I gave the situation a great deal of objective thought.

"At this time I had been married about twenty-five years and not once had my husband ever embarrassed me by looking at other women. Did fame and money and a few sophisticated laughs make up for a very decent man of quiet integrity? No! We were reunited, and it was the best decision I ever made. We had adopted a child and I shudder to think of the adverse influence on her if her parents hadn't been able to harmonize their differences."[5]

The Power of Adoration

My wife thinks I'm a king. She thinks I am the best speaker, the best husband and the best father in the world. Do you know how that affects me? It motivates me to be all that I should be in my relationship with my wife. There is something about the respect she shows me that gives me the desire to become the kind of person others would want me to be. Respect preserves the integrity of the relationship because it creates the desire to protect not only the other person from outside pressures, but the relationship as well. Mutual respect and reverence will take a couple through a lot of hard times and protect against all types of onslaugts on the relationship.

If you are currently dating someone and are considering marriage, I must insist that you ask yourself a very basic question: Do I respect the person I'm seeing? Can I express respect for that individual for the rest of my life because of what that person is or does?

If a sincere yes is your answer, you can use that fact not only to help you determine whether or not you should marry that person, but also to evaluate the genuine maturity level of your love.

Questions to Ponder

- Why are respect and reverence such important ingredients to an intimate marriage relationship?
- What are some ways you can demonstrate reverence and respect for another person?

CHAPTER 18

NO CONDITIONS

It would be impossible for me to describe mature love to you without taking you to the greatest description of love ever penned. The list of qualities which I am about to share with you has appeared in more than just a few modern psychology books. But it originally appeared in the Bible. Let me show you the qualities for a maximum love, sex and marriage relationship as found in 1 Corinthians 13:4-8.

Now please do not think of this familiar passage of Scripture as a definition of love. The only real definition of love found in the Bible is that of Christ's death on the cross. Gary Inrig says it perfectly in his book *Quality Friendship*, when he states, "Love is the action that is consistent with the will and character of God and which, motivated by the character of the lover and the need of the loved, acts without regard to the personal cost for the benefit of another. It is only at the cross that we can see such love, and any definition of love apart from Calvary will be inadequate."[1]

Love Is a Verb

Inrig reminds us that in the original Greek text the words used to describe love are not adjectives, but verbs. This, he explains, is "a deliberate reminder that love is never passive or static. Love is always acting, always moving..."[2]

Kenneth S. Wuest, who brings out the full meaning of each Greek word in his expanded translation of the New Testament, clearly shows that love is active. Here is his translation of 1 Corinthians 13:4-8: "Love meekly and patiently bears ill treatment from others. Love is kind, gentle, benign, pervading, and penetrating the whole nature, mellowing all which would have been harsh and austere; is not envious.

"Love does not brag, nor does it show itself off, is not ostentatious, does not have an inflated ego, does not act unbecomingly, does not seek after the things which are its own, is not irritated, provoked, exasperated, aroused to anger, does not take into account the evil [which it suffers], does not rejoice at the iniquity but rejoices with the truth, endures all things, believes all things, hopes all things, bears up under all things, not losing heart nor courage. Love never fails."[3]

With this kind of love we will stop demanding to have everything our way. We will put no conditions on our love and put the interests and desires of the loved person before our own.

A Transforming Exercise

How do you respond when someone makes a thoughtless comment? Do you ever feel like you've given enough to others, and that it's their turn to give to you for a while?

If your attitudes in any way fall short of biblical love, try reading 1 Corinthians 13:4-8 and inserting "God" for the word "love" ("God is patient, God is kind..."). Now write it out, inserting your name for "love" ("Josh is patient, Josh is kind ..."). Ouch! That really hits home, doesn't it? When the Bible talks about being transformed to the image of Christ, this is what it means. God has high standards.

1 Corinthians 13 is not the final word on love; God's love is shown in countless ways throughout the Bible. However, I challenge you to take the qualities of love found in this passage and make an effort to implement them in your life and in your relationships with others.

No *If's* or *Because's*...Period!

Now, I am going to describe to you three kinds of love. And I want you to use this description as a mirror to evaluate the love relationships you now have with your friends, family, members of the opposite sex, or your spouse.

The first type of love is the only kind many people have ever known. I call it "love if." You and I give or receive this love when certain requirements are met. Our motivation is basically selfish, and our purpose is to gain something in exchange for our love. "If you are a good child, Daddy will love you." "If you meet my expectations as a lover...if you will satisfy my desires...if you will go to bed with me, I will love you."

I've met so many women who know no other type of love than one which says, "I will love you if you put out." Many marriages break up because they were built on this type of love. The husband or wife turns out to be in love with some imaginary, romanticized image. When disillusionment sets in, or expectations cease to be met, "love if" often turns into resentment.

The second type of love (and I think most people marry on the basis of this one) is "love because of." The person is loved because of something he is, has or does. This love is produced by a quality or condition in the person's life. "Love because of" often sounds like this, "I love you because you are pretty;" "I love you because you give me security; because you're so popular," etc.

You may think that "love because of" sounds pretty good. We all want to be loved for certain qualities in our life. Having someone love us because of what we are can initially put us at ease, because we know there is something about us which is lovable. But this type of love soon becomes no better than "love if," a truly shaky foundation for a marriage.

For example, consider the problem of competition. In a "love because of" relationship, what happens when someone comes along with more of the qualities for which you are loved? Suppose you're a woman, and your beauty is one of the hallmarks of your husband's love. What happens when a more beautiful woman comes on the scene? Or suppose you're a man, and your wife's love is based on your salary and the things that come with it. What happens when someone with more money comes along? Will the competition put you on edge? Will it threaten your love? If it will, then yours is a "because of" type of love.

Most of us have two images of ourselves. We are one person on the outside, but we also know we are a deep-down-inside person that few people really know. I have learned that in "love because of" relationships we are afraid to let our partner know what we are really like deep down inside. We are fearful we will be less accepted, less loved or even rejected, if our partner got to know the real us.

Is there anything in your life you cannot share with your partner for fear of even minor discomfort or rejection? If so, I promise you you'll have difficulty experiencing maximum sex, because profound sexual intimacy requires 100 percent trust and giving. The first place any fear or insecurity shows itself is between the sheets.

In a maximum expression of true sexuality we always become completely vulnerable. It is this very openness that makes maximum sexual gratification and sharing possible. This same openness makes possible the deepest sort of hurt if we're not completely accepted. In a "love because of" relationship you can never give of yourself totally in sharing physical love because the risk of being hurt is so great.

This Is It!

I'm happy to say there is still another kind of love. It is love without conditions, or condition-less love. This love says, "I love you in spite of what you may be like deep down inside. I love you no matter what would change about you. I love you, PERIOD!"

Make no mistake. This love isn't blind. It can know fully the other person's shortcomings and faults, yet it totally accepts that individual without demanding anything in return. You can't earn this kind of love, and you can't turn it off. It has no strings attached. It is different from "because of" love in that it isn't based on some attractive quality in the loved person.

"Love, period" can only be experienced by a complete and fulfilled individual—one who doesn't have to take from life's relationships to fill the voids in his or her own life.

As a person who travels a lot, I have seen both Christians and non-Christians experience this third kind of love. But those I have seen experience it over a longer period of time (and that is how I like to judge the quality of something) have not just been Christians, they have been Christ-centered individuals.

As you may recall, I was in my second year at the university when I set out to write my first book, *Evidence That Demands A Verdict*, to make an intellectual joke of Christianity. I thought, *Any fool can do that, and I qualify.* My goal was to put down a few professors who simply irritated me with their talk about Jesus. After two years of research throughout the United States and Europe, it all backfired on me. I realized intellectually that Jesus Christ is who He claimed to be. And I am more certain of that today than ever before.

Christ said, "I stand at the door and knock. If any man hears My voice and opens the door, I will come in." So I invited Christ to come into my life, and in the first six months to a year, He so fulfilled me on the inside that I felt free to give without demanding something in return.

You see, this is the basic difference between "love if" and "love because" on the one hand, and "I love you, period" on the other. Love can't wait to give. Lust can't wait to get. The reason I like to call this third type of love condition-less rather than unconditional is that each of us is restrained and limited by our very nature, which is selfish. Rebellion against God has affected our ability to love unconditionally. Only God through Jesus Christ has demonstrated a total unconditional love. Only through faith in Jesus Christ can we be forgiven and have a personal relationship with our heavenly Father because Christ died on the cross for our sins. Whether you realize it or not, "love, period" is very important to you.

The Possible Dream

If you are not presently experiencing this kind of love, it is likely you are still hoping that someday you will. "Love, period" is spelled G-I-V-E. It is freely giving of yourself. And in this relationship, there's no room for fear, frustration, pressure, envy, or jealousy.

At this point you may be wondering whether this third type of love is practical, or even possible. A woman in England said to me, "If I loved my fiance just the way he is, regardless of what happened, he would care less about how he looks or acts, and our relationship would deteriorate." I replied, "That's where you are wrong." This third attitude toward love is a creative love, one which causes changes in the person receiving it.

During our fourteen years of marriage, my wife has pointed out to me things in my life which, when changed, have enabled me to be a better person, a better husband, a better father, a better representative of Jesus Christ and a better friend. But in our fourteen years of marriage, my wife has never once said to me, "Honey, you have to change!" Instead, she points something out to me, gives me the logic behind it, encourages me in the change, and then she continues loving me. I know that if I never change in that area it will not affect her acceptance of me. Do you know what happens? It is absolutely amazing. Within me arises the desire to change—not because I have to, but because I want to change. Only this third kind of love causes those creative changes.

Let me share with you, in Dottie's own words, why condition-less love motivates her to be better. "I have complete confidence that Josh loves and accepts me just the way I am, yet he encourages me to be better. This sets me free to be me and to try to be even better because I do not feel boxed in or controlled."

Mature love is characterized by unconditional, or more realistically condition-less, acceptance. Not only is it other-person centered, but it also gives us a desire to accept our loved ones just as they are, and not for what they can become or how they can be changed in the future. Put simply, mature love is no more and no less than fully wanting to "get what you see."

Questions to Ponder

- What are some of the problems with "love because of"?
- Explain "condition-less love.
- Why does "condition-less" love motivate us to be better?

FURTHER HELPFUL RESOURCES:
Gary Inrig, *Quality Friendship*, (Chicage, IL: Moody Press, 1981).

CHAPTER 19

JOY IN BEING TOGETHER

One of the greatest tests of love is whether there is pain in being separated from the one loved, and an increase in joy when in that person's presence. Mature love exhibits a tremendous joy in the presence of the other person, and a longing to be together when apart.

I was at Virginia Polytechnical Institute on a Tuesday when a young man came to me for counsel. He was a graduate student there, and his fiancée worked on the staff of another university. He shared with me that they were to be married the following Saturday. But, he explained, "We have already called the wedding off twice—once the week before. My problem is that I really don't know if I love her."

As shaken as this young man was, I could see that his problem was not just a case of pre-marital jitters. And I was amazed that he hadn't figured out months earlier whether or not he loved her. So, I asked him, "Have you ever had a 'long lost weekend'?" He didn't understand, so I explained.

"Thanksgiving is a good example of a 'long lost weekend' where you can visit her, or she can visit you, for about four days—from Wednesday until Sunday. I call it a long lost weekend because you have no recollection of anything that may have happened in the news."

"We've had lots of those weekends," he said.

"O.K.," I continued, "Now, I want to determine what your attitude is like on those weekends."

Two Scenarios

"Let me paint for you two scenarios, and we'll see which one best describes you.

"The first is that two or three weeks before Thanksgiving you begin counting the days, the hours and even the minutes until you can be together. It's Wednesday evening and you're done with school, or you just got off work and you can hardly wait to get there! You jump in your car and take off. (About the only time I ever got speeding tickets was on my way to see Dottie when we were dating.)

"You finally arrive, get a big hug and you feel like you're on top of the world! Thursday and Friday come and go and when Saturday rolls around you don't even want to think about Sunday, because you know that's when you will have to leave. You try to block it out of your mind. On Saturday night you don't want to go to bed because you know that when you get up the next day you will have only a few more hours together. On Sunday you really stretch the hours, but the time just flies. And when you say 'good-bye,' you feel like you are leaving a part of yourself behind.

"Does that sound familiar? Or does this second scenario fit you better?

"You arrive on Wednesday night and everything is great. Thursday and Friday are tremendous. You are having a wonderful time. When Saturday rolls around you are looking forward to Sunday, because you know you need a break. On Sunday you don't really mind too much that you have to leave—it's time for a breather."

Then I asked the student, "Do you look forward to those breathers? Do you feel you need some space?"

He replied, "For a long time, the first scenario fit me. But I have to admit that in the last six to nine months I have looked forward to those breathers."

"In that case," I advised him, "Don't get married. Don't marry someone you can live with. Marry someone you cannot live without. There is a big difference."

A Difference in Longings

Mature love rejoices in togetherness, and that joy doesn't diminish after a few days. In fact, it increases so much that you want to block out of your mind the day you have to separate. Don't get married until, for all the right reasons, you don't want Sunday to come around.

This was one of the major differences between my relationship with Dottie and my relationship with Paula. Paula and I thought we were in love, and those weekends we spent together were fun, but when Sunday came around, I didn't really mind. I was looking forward to a break.

It was different when I dated Dottie. When Thursday came around, I didn't want to think about Friday. On Friday I didn't want Saturday to come, because that was the day before I would have to leave. On Saturday I thought of every possible excuse to stay. When Sunday came, I didn't even set the alarm, thinking if I slept in I wouldn't have to leave.

I remember our first "long lost weekend" at the home of a friend in Houston. On Sunday, she had to fly Braniff to Austin, and I had to go on to a conference in Chicago. As I drove her to the airport, I prayed that Braniff would be late. We stood in the lobby and I kissed her good-bye, and as she walked down the corridor and disappeared into the plane, it was all I could do to hold myself back from running after her and saying, "Don't leave!"

In all the times we were together, joy in the presence of the other increased, and even when we are apart today, there is a longing to be together. By the grace of God, I could live without Dottie, but to be honest, I sure wouldn't want to. I think that is a sign of mature love.

Walter Trobisch, in his sensitive book, *I Loved A Girl*, says you are in love "if you cannot imagine living your life without her; if you feel pain when you are away from her; if she occupies your thoughts, and inspires your dreams at all times; if her happiness means more to you than your own."[1]

Marriage and family counselor Dr. Henry Brandt writes that love is mature when a couple "enjoys being together more than being with anyone else, although others are not excluded from their lives. They discover that each can even have a good time doing something together which neither would enjoy doing alone. When they are absent from each other, each is in the background of the other's thoughts."[2] The old cliché, "Absence makes the heart grow fonder," is more indicative of mature love than most people realize.

Tougher Every Time

My ministry takes me on the road 50 percent of my time. Although my family accompanies me sometimes, I am away from Dottie and the kids at least twelve days a month. You might assume it would get easier after fifteen years, but it just gets harder. Some men come to me after having spent a weekend away from their wives and tell me, "It was tough. I don't know how you do it, I could never be away from my wife and kids for a longer period of time." They add, "But I guess you get used to it." That tends to ruffle my feathers—I never get used to it. And I don't ever want to. When love is mature and deep, you desperately try to squeeze a ten-day trip into nine, always striving to be together.

Dottie is often confronted about my travel time away. Well-meaning and caring people express their sympathy and encouragement, saying they hope I'll be home more in the future. Dottie explains her feelings and responds, "I never love to see him leave for a trip, but I am committed to what he is doing. In a sense there is a grieving process every time he has to leave, because I miss him. There's an emptiness that can't be filled by anything else. But because we are committed to what he is doing, it's a choice we have made. Choices aren't always easy, but they are necessary. I believe in this choice so much that I let him do what he needs to do—what God has called him to do—and I do what God has called me to do.

"It's not that I love it when he walks through the door to leave. I'm the type of person who could very easily become dependent on him. I've had to be somewhat independent and make some independent decisions, which is very good for me. But it's not easy, and being apart is not something you can ever get used to.

"I'm proud of what he does and what we do as a team, even though it means a little bit of inconvenience for both of us. There is a joy in being with him, and there is a joy in not being with him, because I know that what he is doing is what God wants him to do, and that he is able to exercise the incredible gift God has given him."

Mature love can make the choice to be apart, although it may not be easy.

Questions to Ponder

- If you are currently involved in a serious dating relationship, apply the "long lost weekend" test.
- In your case, does absence make the heart grow fonder?

CHAPTER 20

BEING REALISTIC

It may be true that marriages are made in heaven, but they are lived out here on earth between imperfect people. When love is mature it takes this into account and is realistic in its expectations. If your love for someone is mature, you will love and accept that person just as he or she is—shortcomings and all—and not for what you hope he or she will become.

This kind of mature love, however, always encounters several barriers to seeing an individual or a relationship realistically.

Idealistic fantasies about our marriage and mate is the first barrier usually encountered.

"The most dangerous person to marry," writes Evelyn Duvall, "is your ideal—dangerous because you are likely to overlook the presence of disqualifying defects or the absence of character essentials."[1]

Someone has said that marriage will cut your sorrows in half, double your joy, and could well triple your expenses. In his zeal for marriage, however, the man who thinks he has found his ideal may find it easy to excuse her shortcomings. The woman who approaches a relationship wearing rose-colored glasses will have a distorted view of the man she marries. This always forms a barrier to experiencing a true and mature love.

Author Charles Swindoll touches on reality in relationships when he observes, "There is no such thing as a home completely without conflicts. The last couple to live 'happily ever after' was Snow White and Prince Charming. Even though you are committed to your mate, there will still be times of tension, tears, struggle, disagreement, and impatience. Commitment doesn't erase our humanity! That's bad news, but it's realistic."[2]

When one falls in love with a fantasy or idealized image, one of two results is usually forthcoming: Either the spouse is rejected for not measuring up to the image, or a concerted effort is made to change him or her into that image.

Rollercoaster Feelings

A desire for constant feelings and passions is a second obstacle to realistic love. Mature love is not just a strong feeling. It is a commitment, a promise, a pledge. Feelings will come and go, but love remains constant. Don't become confused if you're not always bubbly with feelings of love, and don't give up on the relationship the first time either of you thinks the feelings are cooling off. Realistic love is prepared for these times and uses them to strengthen, rather than to weaken, the relationship.

My mate will fulfill all my needs all of the time is a third barrier to realism in love. This commonly held fallacy trips up many a couple. Many people are looking for that certain someone who can understand them fully and give them everything they feel is missing in their lives.

What often happens in such cases is that a man meets a woman who satisfies some of his most acute needs, which he then exaggerates in his mind to encompass *all* of his needs. He thinks he has found the "right one" who fulfills his every desire, when in fact he has found someone who happens to fulfill a few key areas of his life. He actually overlooks the needs that have not been satisfied. And what he is really saying to her is, "I love you *only* because you take care of needs in my life and you fulfill my expectations."

One writer put it this way, "It is probably impossible for any two people to completely fulfill one another's needs. If a pair could mutually satisfy even eighty percent of one another's needs, it would be a minor miracle. The expectation of total need fulfillment within a marriage ruins many marital relationships."[3]

Details...Details

In my own marriage I have discovered many instances in which I did not meet Dottie's needs or emotions. As I described earlier, she expected me to be interested in the finer details of her story, when in fact the details don't always register with me. As she now explains it, "It bothered me more when we were first married, but I have come to see that I can't expect him to be someone he's not. He can't always meet every single need I have. If he could, he would be God. He realizes that I can't meet every last need of his either, but I do the best I can.

"If I thought Josh wasn't listening, I would feel like he wasn't making an effort to understand me. When he doesn't hang on every word of my story, I have the choice of feeling hurt or realizing that this is his temperament and personality.

"I am the kind of person who will listen to every detail of a story. He is the kind of person whose mind clicks on to other things after too many details because they're just not necessary to him. Since I understand who he is and what he is made of, I can be realistic in our relationship. I would like him to soak in all of the details, but that's not his style, and I can't expect more of him than who he is."

Psychologist Dr. Larry Crabb explains why we are unable to meet all of our spouse's needs:

"The most accepting wife in the world cannot meet her husband's need for significance. Because she is a sinner, my wife will not always minister to me as she should; even if she were to do so, she does not have the power to make me adequate for an eternally important task— and that alone will satisfy me.

"The most loving husband in the world can never meet his wife's need for security. The stain of self-centeredness has discolored every motivation within us. We are utterly incapable of providing our wives with the unconditional and selfless acceptance they require. We simply are not enough for each other."[4]

A husband or wife can fulfill certain desires, but there are others that only God can take care of. And forcing a spouse into the role of having to meet every need produces conflict and will destroy the relationship. As Christians we know that we are complete in Christ and that there is nothing in our lives He can't handle, yet so often we expect our mates to play God for us. We need to realize that our mates' inability to fulfill us entirely is a gift from God—it keeps us looking to Him.

Promises...Promises

Promises of change which are usually contingent on an event or a period of time are still another barrier to viewing a person or relationship realistically. How many people have said, "Don't worry, honey, when we get married, I'll stop drinking," or, "Believe me, once we're married, I'll stop fooling around behind your back"?

Now I want you to mark my word. There is nothing in that person's promise or character that is worth believing. The promises will never end. "Once we have our first child, I'll quit drinking for sure...Once I get that promotion...Once we have our own place..." and so on.

Don't base your relationship on promises. Get it straightened out beforehand. It is the relationship as it stands now that counts.

If you want your mate truly to think of you as a trustworthy person, you have to be trustworthy now. If you want your mate to see you as a man or woman of God, you have to be one now. If all of the events in your life up to this point haven't caused you to stop drinking, what makes you think some magical event in the future will? Realism in the relationship is lost when it is based on promises.

A desire to change the other person is a fifth obstacle to a realistic evaluation of a loved one—"I'll put an end to that once we're married!" This is similar to the problem of promises, except in this case one spouse is taking it upon himself or herself to mold the other. "He just needs a little time. I can change him after we've settled down." Simple common sense dictates that time to settle down and change should be given him before the *I do's* are rehearsed.

You Get More of What You See

Be sure you love a person for who he or she is, not for what you imagine or want the person to become. I have lost count of the people I have counseled who thought they could change someone once they became married to them. The key phrase to remember is: *What you are as a single person, you will be as a married person, only to a greater degree.* Any negative character trait will be intensified in a marriage relationship, because you will feel free to let your guard down—that person has committed himself to you, and you no longer have to worry about scaring him off.

The couple that frequently argues or is unable to work out differences will not find life any better after marriage.

"You can't make someone over," warns Dr. Herman Weiss. "You won't be able to make him more romantic, wittier, more outgoing, less of a gambler/drinker/smoker, or even cure his allergy to your cat. You cannot afford to become his mother, his teacher or his therapist. Look before you leap into a relationship."[5]

A woman might fall in love with a man because she wants to believe he is everything he says he is. The problem is that a lot of men talk a good fight but can't deliver once they're in the ring. Mature love doesn't talk big or believe in big talk. If your love is mature, you won't kid yourselves about each other.

Dottie knew what she was getting into when she married me. She knew that God had called me to a ministry as a speaker, and she didn't kid herself about what kind of a life that can be. She said, "When I committed myself to Josh, I committed myself to him totally as a person and totally to the fact that he is a speaker. With that comes the reality of a great deal of travel, which means we cannot always be together.

"When we considered marriage, I was confronted with the travel issue. I had to face and work through that before I could make an intelligent decision on marriage.

"People will say, 'Oh, isn't that too bad that you're apart so much? Don't you wish he didn't have to travel?' I sometimes react to that kind of statement, because Josh is not abandoning me. No one has any idea what has gone into a decision for him to travel—it's not a flippant decision. We make that choice.

"I think I can handle the travel now because God prepared me beforehand. I was single and on staff of Campus Crusade for Christ at the University of Texas when I heard Josh speak for the first time. I had never heard him before, and I was profoundly influenced by what he said, and I used to go around quoting him, 'This famous speaker says...' (One of my favorite quotes was 'Peace is not the absence of conflict, but the ability to cope with conflict.' I used that one a lot.)

"I was very impressed with his ministry and the impact he had on our campus, although I had no idea I would later marry him, and he didn't even know I was alive.

"Later, when we were still dating, I had the wonderful opportunity to travel with him to the University of Tennessee. I was able to see his ministry from a different perspective and see how he affects the lives of students and staff. So I had both prepared for his coming to a campus and been with him as he went to a campus. I saw the incredible work that goes into his speaking trips—the preparation, the homework, the late hours, the exhaustion, the hectic schedules, sleeping in a different bed every night, and so on. That gave me a well-balanced understanding of his ministry before we were ever married.

"I stand behind Josh 100 percent, because I feel God has equipped him uniquely to share with people around the world about how they can know Christ personally and walk with Him in their everyday lives.

"I have shared this to show that in dealing with the travel aspect of Josh's life, I looked at it from all perspectives so that I could realistically understand it. I needed to evaluate that situation in light of my love for him, what he does and what God has called me to do.

"Since we dealt with this problem and 'headed it off at the pass' from the beginning of our relationship, it has not become a sore spot in our marriage. In fact, it has become a blessing as we work out the scheduling together and see God work."

Love Isn't Blind

One of the most subtle barriers to realistically evaluating a relationship is the overly accepted cliché, "Love is blind." This attitude shows up in phrases like, "Look, you love her, right? Then don't worry about those things," or, "Go ahead, get married; it'll work out. It always does!" Divorce statistics show that more than half of the time it just doesn't work out, and that willfully overlooking potential points of conflict is an invitation to disaster.

Some people will joke that marriage is a "leap in the dark by the light of the moon." Others say you can be in "love at first sight." Let me suggest you take a second look before you leap. Often the lover becomes so enmeshed in dreams and ideals that the loved one is not a real person, merely a composite of the lover's desires. The blind love may ignore the other's shortcomings for a while, but it can't last forever.

If your love is blind, you're bound to trip sooner or later. If you love the total person, you don't kid yourself about him or her. Mature love seeks out and deals with all aspects of the person, both the positive and the negative, and means understanding with your mind that you can love this person for better or for worse.

True, there are candlelights and kisses, but there is also the laundry and the grocery shopping and two people trying to operate in one bathroom in the morning. There are long, romantic walks and hair to run your fingers through, but there are also wrinkles and pimples. Love is blind when we see and accept the other as anything less than a total person.

One woman said that realistic acceptance of a man means "loving a man today for who and what he is, not for what you would like to help him to become tomorrow." This does not mean, of course, that she's blind to her husband's shortcomings; it only means that she accommodates them. "Truthfully, I wouldn't change him at all," she wrote. "I *would* give him the gift of tact, if I could. He is such an up-front type of guy that I can't believe he is doing so well in politics. He is strictly, 'What you see is what you get.' "[6]

Marriage is two imperfect individuals coming together in a relationship. Mature love is unconditional commitment to an imperfect person.

Fatal Exaggerations

In *American Ways Of Love*, Frank Cox writes, "Often we project our beliefs onto another person, exaggerating those characteristics that match the qualities we are looking for and masking those that do not. That is, we transform the other person into an unreal hero or heroine to fit our personal concept of the romantic marital partner. In essence, we often fall in love with our own romantic ideas rather than with a real human being.

"Those who 'fall in love' in this way will suffer disappointment when the real person of their chosen partner begins to emerge. Rather than meet this emerging person with joy and enthusiasm, partners who hold romanticized ideals may reject reality in favor of their stereotypic images. They may again commence to search for the proper object of their love, rejecting the real-life partner as unworthy or changed."[7]

Realistic Steps

Although the obstacles to a realistic evaluation of a relationship are great, you can overcome them. By taking certain positive steps, you can better determine the status of the relationship and your understanding of the other person.

One step is to ask yourself some hard, down-to-earth questions:

Why do I want to marry him/her? Is it for money, security, status, or any other such reason? Is it an escape? Is it because I think it will solve my problems? How would I feel toward this person if something happened and he/she were no longer rich or good looking?

Do you communicate? Do you stimulate each other's minds? Or does one of you find the other intellectually boring? Do you have the same general goals and interests? Are you on the same wavelength in your spiritual walks? Do you like each other's friends? (That says a great deal.) How do your attitudes concerning children, finances, in-laws, really match up?

What are his/her shortcomings or weaknesses? What are yours? What don't you like about him/her? Why? What do you think he/she doesn't like about you? And, why?

If you think you're going to spend the rest of your life with this person, you had better break into a big smile at the thought. If you aren't ready to take this person as he or she now is, then please reassess your position. You have to be able to accept the other as a real person, complete with faults, and be able to deal with your differences in a godly and accepting manner.

Mature and realistic love realizes that partners in a relationship have different perspectives in many areas, and loves that person for who he is, not for what he has to offer.

Know Your Expectations

Another positive step is to share your expectations of each other and of the marriage. This will keep you from the disastrous results of going into a marriage with unrealistic expectations and a distorted image of the other person. Learn as much as you can about each other to give your relationship the most solid base possible.

Marriage counselor and author Dr. H. Norman Wright describes the value of transparency in discussing marriage expectations when he writes, "Each individual enters marriage with both an overt and a hidden set of expectations for the marriage and the partner's behavior and performance. As the marriage proceeds, some are brought to the surface and some linger beneath. When these expectations are all brought into the open, evaluated, challenged and discussed, greater harmony comes to the marriage. 'And he shall be like a tree firmly planted [and tended] by the streams of water, ready to bring forth his fruit in its season; his leaf also shall not fade or wither, and everything he does shall prosper [and come to maturity]' (Psalm 1:3, Amplified)."[8]

Voicing hopes and expectations is a very healthy practice in a relationship because it allows each partner to appraise himself properly in light of the desires of the other, and to see if each is able to meet the needs of the other. Speaking up also allows possible areas of conflict to surface long before the situation arises, and allows each person to become better prepared to understand the other's point of view in the conflict. At the same time, the couple will discover areas of compatibility and common interest never before discussed.

One woman described how sharing expectations with her (future) husband had helped to clarify areas that were sources of friction. "Most adjustments were in terms of how to best communicate and understand each other, because any time you have two people who want to get married, you have different sexes (of course), different families, different educational backgrounds, differences in cultural backgrounds, and on and on. Suddenly you have to make all of this into one, and you discover you have different perspectives on all kinds of things. And for some reason I guess I didn't expect us to have those different perspectives.

"Somehow I thought that once we got married, magic would be sprinkled on us and we would always agree. Talking out our expectations in advance showed us a lot. That was the beginning of my realizing that we weren't always going to agree, but I think what hit me the most was how different our expectations really were. That's the kind of stuff you need to know."

Tough Advice

Brad and Margy are like many couples, struggling through differences and pre-marriage jitters, who come to me for counsel. I told them, "I'm not sure if you should get married. That's a decision you two will have to make. But let me encourage you, as you evaluate your relationship and love for each other, to face openly and honestly all doubts and fears in these areas. Realize that these misgivings may have no basis in fact, but don't ignore them. By dealing with uneasy feelings you will either strengthen your relationship or discover that you're not right for each other.

"Secondly, I want to affirm the value of marriage when you've found the right person! Marriage is a wonderful blessing, but it is too important to enter into with doubts. It's natural to have some fears about beginning a lifelong commitment to a marriage, but if your feelings are more than just the usual pre-marital jitters, don't get married right now—give it time.

"The worst possible thing you two could do is ignore those unsure feelings or pretend they don't exist. I've seen too many people get hurt because they went ahead with marriage without resolving doubts. I've also seen God salvage marriages that seemed strained beyond repair. The problem is, most people are not willing to compromise their demands and let Him work in their lives.

"I thank God for Dottie and the relationship we have, but I know that for two people who aren't right for each other marriage can be a catastrophe."

Avoiding Spiritual Cop-outs

Mature love is open-eyed and realistic. Unfortunately, many couples try to over-spiritualize the relationship in an attempt to mask their doubts. Emphasizing the spiritual aspect of the relationship in an attempt to ignore day-to-day difficulties is a cop-out.

Before you can approach your future mate with your expectations, you have to know what they are. The best way to understand your own thinking is to write everything down. Write down your expectations for yourself, your marriage, your spouse, your future and anything else that comes to mind. When each of you has done this, you can come together with an attitude of anticipation and curiosity. This is your chance to find out what that person really wants out of life, and whether or not the two of you are headed down the same road. The more realistically you view that person now, the stronger the foundation will be if you get married.

Questions to Ponder

- What are obstacles to realistic love?
- Which one is present in your life?
- What tough questions do you need to ask yourself about your expectations?

FURTHER HELPFUL RESOURCES:
Josh McDowell, *Evidence for Joy*, (Word Books).

CHAPTER 21

A PROTECTIVE ATTITUDE

I am constantly amazed at what people say about their spouse in public. It makes me wonder what they say to each other in private. In front of his wife, one man said to me, "Let me tell you, there are few people who cook like my wife, but the Army comes close." And you've probably winced as I have at the dinner party classic when the meal doesn't turn out, "Aw, you'll never make another Betty Crocker."

True love doesn't make remarks like these. Mature love manifests itself in a protective attitude. And if negative remarks occur, mature love will immediately repent and seek forgiveness.

If your love is mature, you will think of the other person first, and you will want to protect that person in public as well as in private. When the other person's happiness, security and development have become as important as your own, you will want to shield that person from any harm.

One woman shared how her husband began to belittle her in public.

"Just teasing," he said. "Can't you take it?"

"I was stunned, hurt and humiliated," she confessed.

In my home, I can assure you if you want to criticize me in a negative way don't do it in front of my wife. She loves me and has a very protective attitude. She will put you in your place.

After a talk I gave at a church in Alaska the town antagonist, who frequently appeared at the church, marched to the front and started hurling accusations at me. I remained calm—while my wife wanted to grab an umbrella near her and chase the man out. She recalls that she was so furious that two people had to restrain her. She wanted to protect me. Norman Wright has wisely observed that "marriage resembles a pair of shears, so joined that they cannot be separated; often moving in opposite directions, yet always punishing anyone who comes

183

between them."[1]

Taking the Defense

I am also protective of Dottie in a different, but very practical way. I protect her from the children when they act disrespectfully toward her. Dottie recently shared, "He is constantly building me up with my children and telling them what a neat mom they have. I need to hear and feel his support in the programs that I am pursuing with them, and in the things that I'm trying to teach them. One thing Josh does that shows me that he's on my side, and how much he loves me, is to always come to my rescue immediately when one of the children shows any sign of disrespect.

"When we were first married I picked up a book on marriage and read how the father protects the mother from the children. I scratched my head and thought, what is he talking about? It made no sense to me. But, years later, when one of the kids sassed me, Josh marched right up and said, 'You might talk to your mother that way, but don't let me ever hear you talk to my wife that way!' The children understood, and it quit.

"At that point Josh was protecting me from a child's immaturity and accusations, one of the wonderful things a father can do for a mother—he protects her from a child that is unruly at that moment. This is a benefit to the mother, because she knows that her husband supports her; it is a benefit to the child because he or she realizes that the two parents will stand together."

Author Harold J. Sala offers good advice in his article, "20 Commandments For A Better Marriage": Thou shalt not let anyone criticize thy wife to thy face and get away with it.[2] Protecting your mate doesn't mean you are blind to your loved one's shortcomings and faults. It does mean, however, shielding and protecting your spouse from both verbal and physical abuse.

When you know your loved one will protect you and come to your defense, you will become more trusting and vulnerable, more intimate and caring.

Questions to Ponder

- What does it mean to have a protective attitude toward a loved one?
- In what ways can you protect the one you love?
- What are some positive results of demonstrating a protective attitude?

22

TAKE RESPONSIBILITY

Remember the husband committed to basketball and baseball—and his friends? What did you think of his behavior? I'm sure you were outraged, like I was, for mature love accepts responsibility!

Real love always translates into real concern for the other person, showing a willingness to take on responsibilities concerning family, finances, health, children. If you do not believe that your mate is taking responsiblity in your relationship, you will never be able to give yourself totally to that person.

Conversely, when you know your partner does take real responsibility for your love, you become truly free to love that person with abandon. This total abandonment to the other person in a maximum love, marriage and sex relationship is what God designed for us to enjoy. It's our spiritual calling. But it is unattainable if one or both of the partners are irresponsible.

"In an age of 'do your own thing,'" write the Lees in *The Total Couple*, "responsibility has become a dirty word. We are told at every turn that there is no need to feel guilty when throwing off responsibilities for our own greater good. How insensitive. Truth is that anyone giving up a set of responsibilities must, if he or she cares about others, feel some guilt for forcing change…the guilt should not stop us from living our own lives; it should only stop us from unnecessarily hurting the lives of others."[1]

Sex and Responsibility

If your mate doesn't consistently demonstrate responsiblity, you will always hold back in the relationship and never be totally trusting. So many today want sex without responsibility and intimacy without commitment; it's no wonder they feel robbed and empty in their sex lives. Sex was created to be expressed within the context of commitment and responsibility.

Dr. Betty Hamburg, a research psychiatrist at the National Institute of Mental Health, says about youth, "We've speeded up the clock without being very helpful to adolescents. We teach them about Fallopian tubes but very little about the meaning of relationships and responsibility toward others."[2]

Dr. Walter Trobisch in *I Loved A Girl* points out, "True love involves responsibility—the one for the other and both before God. Where love is, you no longer say 'I,' but 'you'; 'I am responsible for you. You are responsible for me.' Together then you stand before God where you do not say 'You and I,' but rather 'we.' "[3]

Without responsibility, a marriage union is merely two self-centered individuals entering into a self-centered relationship. Mature love involves responsibility and dependability. "Unfinished jobs, broken promises, and unfulfilled good intentions," writes Strauss, "are examples of *un*dependability.

"An immature person cannot happily perform the tasks for which he is responsible. He grumbles and complains, finding no satisfaction or enjoyment in a job well done. Housewives grumble because life is dull and routine. Working mothers long to be full-time homemakers. Men hop from job to job in quick, haphazard decisions that fail to include their wives. Some men overlook the common courtesy of phoning their wives when they cannot come home at the expected time. The fruit of the Spirit is faith, a word meaning 'faithfulness' or 'dependability.' We need to yield to the Spirit and grow up to faithfulness!"[4]

Questions to Ponder

- What happens in a relationship when there is no sense of responsibility?
- What happens when both partners take responsibility for themselves, as well as for the relationship?

CHAPTER 23

DEMONSTRATED BY COMMITMENT

What kind of commitment did you build into your marriage vows? Did you include "until death do us part"? If you did, you are in a minority. Commitment is hardly a buzzword these days.

Our "throw-away" culture seems intent on throwing out the principle of commitment in relationships. Dr. Robert Taylor, author of the book, *Couples—The Art Of Staying Together*, said, "We're now living in the age of disposability: Use it once, and throw it away. Over the past decade, there has developed a feeling that relationships are equally disposable."[1] Yet a hallmark of mature love is commitment.

I have come to believe that most couples are defeated even before they marry. They enter into marriage with the attitude, "If it doesn't work, or if we have problems, we will simply dispose of it." This shallow view of commitment is best described by the phrases "out of sight, out of mind," and "if you're not with the one you love, love the one you're with." There is no place for such self-centered attitudes in a truly Christian love, sex and marriage relationship. Mature love says, "If I'm not with the one I love, I'm going to wait."

In responding to the question, "Do you think the so-called 'me' society leads to more broken marriages?" Dr. Robert Taylor said, "Yes. I believe the 'me' philosophy is contributing to the high divorce rate we now have. The problem goes back to the child-rearing principles that were in effect from the mid-40s to the mid-60s. This was considered to be the age of permissiveness, when wants became needs and parents failed to teach their children how to deal with frustration. They failed to teach them a sense of commitment to relationships and to others.

Many people in the group are now young adults in the early years of marriage, when they are most vulnerable to divorce."[2]

The Other Side of the Coin

Not surprisingly, sacrifice has fallen on the same hard times as commitment. Yet without sacrifice, commitment is meaningless. Sacrifice is the mouthpiece of commitment. We know our mate is committed when he or she is willing to sacrifice on our behalf, not only by what he or she says, but by what is done as well. Unless you are sure that your mate is committed to the relationship and is willing to sacrifice for it, you cannot abandon yourself to the other person as God intended. You will always be holding back. As a result, you will be robbed of the intimacy and oneness in the relationship you were designed to enjoy.

The prevalent attitude that, "I'll work at the relationship as long as there is something in it for me," is absolutely destructive. Instead of jumping ship when the going gets tough, a mature kind of love is willing to stay and work out the problem. Studies show that commitment is essential for couples to deal successfully with problems and frustrations. Research indicates that when a couple demonstrate commitment to each other, mutual attraction grows—the perception of the mate changes, and the individuals become more loving toward one another.

One such study reveals that a growing commitment and the willingness to sacrifice and work on the relationship is the key to long-term, happy marriages. Dr. Charles Swindoll, host of the popular radio program, "Insight For Living," and his wife Cynthia declare their commitment to each other several times a year. He says, "We get alone, often for an overnight somewhere cozy and private. While there, we look at each other and verbalize our promise to remain faithful. We actually declare aloud our commitment. We can't explain how or why it works, but there's something reassuring about putting things like that into words. As our ears hear what our mouths are saying (from our hearts, actually), our loyalty is reaffirmed."[3]

I recently felt the need to reverbalize my commitment to my wife. I told her that if I had to do it all over again, I would choose her without a moment's hesitation. When your mate knows that you have that kind of commitment to the relationship and to him or her, there is a greater feeling of security and closeness.

Why is it so important to be committed to working through problems, rather than just walking away from the relationship? Chuck Swindoll lists the following reasons:

1. It is the continual counsel of Scripture.
2. One's growth in Christ is strengthened.
3. The testimony of Christ before the public is enhanced.
4. Working through forces needed changes. To walk out means we take our same hangups into the next relationship.

5. Children in the family remain secure, stable, and balanced. They also learn to run if parents run...or work out the difficulties if that's what mom and dad model.[4]

Let there be no doubt: Mature love is characterized by a commitment that is willing to sacrifice.

Questions to Ponder

- How can you demonstrate commitment to the one you love?
- What happens to a relationship when commitment is demonstrated?
- Why is it important to be committed to work through problems?

24

DYNAMIC GROWTH

Like aerobic conditioning, love is not static. The love shared in a maximum marriage and sex relationship is either growing or atrophying. And a mature kind of love will continue to experience dynamic growth.

Early in our marriage I was speaking on economics to about 300 members of faculty and administration at the University of Tennessee. As I usually do during the first few minutes of the talk, I made some comments about my wife. After all, whatever is most on your heart will also be most on your lips.

In any case, I thought they were very appropriate comments. Suddenly a young professor in his late twenties interrupted my talk and asked in a sarcastic tone of voice, "How long have you been married?"

"Six months," I replied. He then made a sad statement I've heard many times, "Let's see how you talk after you've been married for five years!"

Just You Wait

Before I became engaged I was already speaking on the secret of loving, and people would say, "Let's see how you talk when you're engaged!" Then their comments changed—they told me to just wait until I was married. After I was married, they said I'd change my tune after five years, and then after ten, and then after twenty.

I was sure these people were wrong. My philosophy, however, has always been that a man with experience has an advantage over a man with an argument. So, standing in front of this audience at the University of Tennessee, it seemed that the professor had the advantage of experience. It was one of few times in my life when I've been at a loss for words.

Just then a man in the back stood up and walked up to the front.

He was about seventy-five years old. I didn't know him, and for all I knew he was really going to let me have it. But I learned later he was Roger Rusk, a dynamic Christian, highly respected professor at the university and brother of former Secretary of State Dean Rusk.

He walked to the front row and looked me square in the eyes. Then he turned toward the vocal professor, leaned over, and said, "Mister, it gets better after fifty-five years!" I was incredibly relieved. That incident emphasized to me one of the main qualities of mature love—it does not remain stagnant. If your love is mature, it will grow. If it is not, it will dissipate.

Four Stages of Growth

A number of research studies now demonstrate that a fulfilled marriage is a growing, changing relationship. These studies indicate that a couple's relationship will pass through four basic stages of growth.

In the first stage, "spouses are typically self-centered, looking only at how the relationship can serve them. At the next level they negotiate *quid pro quos*—a service for a service, a concession for a concession. During the third stage they begin to appreciate each other's individuality and make accommodations for the good of the marriage and each other. By the fourth stage they have evolved a set of 'rules of the relationship' by which they can avoid or deal with problems. 'Unfortunately, many marriages are stuck in stage two,' notes Dr. Ronald Levant, a Boston University professor and family therapist. 'The husband and wife never get beyond saying, "I'll wash your back if you wash mine." ' "[1]

If you have a love that is basically unconditional—a love that accepts the other person as is, yet encourages improvement—you're going to have growth. Add to this a commitment to the relationship and a trust factor that leads to meaningful, intimate communication, and you have *dynamic* growth. And this growth leads to deeper feelings and greater caring on the part of each partner.

If you have a best friend—someone you know deeply and intimately—you probably liked that person the first time you met. You felt like, "Wow, there's a chemistry here. We really hit it off and we really enjoy each other." Then over the years, you developed more history together and more "water under the bridge," so that you love the person even more because you're more knowledgeable. The more time that passes, the more your affection for them grows. This same dynamic is true with the Lord. At the time when you become a Christian, you are so in love with Him you can hardly stand it. And as time passes, the feelings deepen.

Take a good look at your relationship. Do you see growth? Especially, if you are engaged, do you see a deepening of your feelings? Your commitment? Your trust? Your ability to communicate on the most intimate level of your feelings? If your love is a mature love, it will be obvious by the tremendous growth you can see in your relationship.

Questions to Ponder

- At what stage of growth are you in your relationship?
- What can you do to experience more growth?

CHAPTER 25

CREATIVE

I know what you're thinking, "This test for mature love isn't fair. I'm not a creative person." Well, relax. Artistic creativity as you're thinking of it isn't the requirement here. Rather, mature love is creative in the way it shows respect and reverence for the other person. It is sensitive to the other person's needs and will therefore find ways to express itself creatively. Mature love seeks out opportunities and unique ways to say "I love you" to the object of its affections.

One creative way I show Dottie that I love her is very practical. I help her with the children. As a mother of three, she is on call twenty-four hours a day. When the children were little, I helped change diapers. Now I often take them out for breakfast to give her some time to herself. When I am home, I try hard to find creative ways to relieve her of some of her duties around the house to show her that I love her.

Dottie is quite creative as well. I remember one time in particular when she visited her parents, and I stayed home. One evening I opened the ice box, and in it I found a note that said, "I love you, honey." When I went to my closet and started to pack, there was a note pinned to every one of my sports jackets. I found a note stuck in my shoes, one was pinned on the towel, and a message in lipstick written on the mirror. It was thrilling!

When we are away on trips, I try to give her time to herself. Dottie has a close friend who lives in Tampa, Florida, and when we recently had to fly to New Orleans, her friend was able to fly in to meet us. She and Dottie spent twenty-four hours together while I took care of the children. It was my creative way of saying "I love you."

Give Love Coupons

One of Dottie's favorite things is a "love coupon." She explains,

"Josh often leaves 'love coupons' around the house when he leaves for a trip. On these certificates he promises to take me to a movie, or to take me out to dinner, or just to give me a hug. I can redeem them when he returns. I'll find them attached to my towel rack, or maybe on the sliding door to the shower, or on my pillow. The coupon that requires the most sacrifice is when he promises to take me to the ballet, since he's not real crazy about that!"

Now, if I were to give you a list of the creative things Dottie and I do to show our love, I might rob you of the joy of thinking them up for yourself. All you have to do is look for a need in the other person's life. It can be as practical as giving her a short vacation from the kids, or as much fun as buying him something with money you planned to spend on yourself. If your love is mature and growing, you will never run out of ideas. The best kind of creativity usually costs nothing.

Questions to Ponder

- What are creative ways you can show another person you love him/her? Follow through on your ideas.
- Why do you think it is important to continually and creatively show your love for another person?
- What creative expression of love is present in your relationship?
- What can you do this week to express your love more creatively?

CHAPTER **26**

CONCLUSION

You aren't the first person to search for "the secret of loving." The search for the right marriage partner has led scores of researchers to produce hundreds of articles and books. I have quoted extensively from many of these and footnoted the sources to help you find the information most useful to you.

My real goal, however, is to see you ultimately enjoying a secure marriage that is pleasing both to you and to God. I know what it's like to experience a marriage that is joyful and fulfilling. I wish everyone did. I honestly believe it is possible for every marriage to be a blessing and a success.

Obviously, you won't wake up some morning and discover that your marriage is suddenly fulfilling. A maximum marriage relationship takes a lot of work, both before and after you exchange rings. I know from personal experience.

And not only that, there will be times when it seems like you personally are making all of the effort. You may find yourself giving, yet not receiving; forgiving, yet not being forgiven; loving the other unconditionally as a total person, yet not being totally accepted. Why bother, you might ask? Well, you should bother for one simple reason — *it's worth it.*

We easily forget, but please try to remember that marriage is a lifelong learning process. If your spouse seems content to leave the relationship where it is or to let it drift, he or she is the real loser, not you.

Both you and your mate were made in the image of God—the God who so loved the world. He created within every one of us—He built right into our lives—a desire to love and to respond to love. And when someone gives to us, we become aware that they are reaching out to us and it makes us want to give back. When someone accepts us, even with our faults, we realize that we are loved for who we are and it makes us want to love others just as they are.

If you are putting 100 percent into a relationship but not getting much back, please don't quit. I believe the other person *will* respond. God made us that way.

Irresistible Love

Maybe this is one reason so many people reject Christ. They just can't believe that someone they don't even know could love them so much that He would give His life to make it possible for them to stand completely forgiven before God. Since most of us have never seen love to that degree, it seems beyond our comprehension, and it is easy to reject what we cannot comprehend.

A person may reject the gospel and never give it a second thought. But it is much more difficult, even impossible, to ignore a tangible person's love, especially one who lives under the same roof. The woman who cannot fathom Christ's forgiveness can *see* forgiveness in her husband. And it is this authentic interaction here in time and space that can bring about a response. As I stated earlier, when you give 100 percent, you get back 150 percent.

No Exceptions

Every quality needed to be the "right person" and every aspect of mature love applies to everyone. Whether you have been married for thirty years or are still looking forward to your first date, you need to establish in your life the character and principles necessary to build a lasting and godly marriage.

Perhaps you feel that some of what I have covered is unnecessary. What's the big deal about a clear conscience anyway? Who says I have to be creative in how I love my mate? If you think any of the personal qualities or aspects of mature love I've discussed are not really necessary in a relationship, you should examine the basis of your reasoning. It may be that you are seeing undesirable characteristics of yourself or of your relationship, and you just don't want to deal with them.

Problems in marriages don't go away on their own. You need to resolve the areas of friction by approaching them head-on, honestly and always in love. And if the best and most direct solution to the problem is for you to swallow your pride and ask for forgiveness, do it! I've lost count of the lifeless marriages I have seen revived because one person took it upon himself or herself to make the first move in reconciliation. If your marriage is not alive and exciting or is in need of reconciliation, do something about it. The benefits you will reap in rekindled love and a vibrant marriage are beyond description.

The Real Secret

The key phrase is this: *Seek to improve yourself and seek the best interests of the other*. This is the secret of being the right person and ultimately the secret of loving. Most people approach it the other way around. And if you have ever wondered why one in two marriages now end in divorce, that's the reason.

Seek to improve yourself. Psalm 119:11 says, "Thy word I have treasured in my heart, that I may not sin against Thee." The psalmist sought wisdom from the Word of God. When he found it, he committed it to memory, *not* so that he could go around improving others, but so that he could do right before God.

Seek the best interest of the other person. In Matthew 25 Jesus gives His definition of a righteous people. The righteous, His followers, are those who give of what they have, materially and otherwise, who reach out to recognize the needs of others and meet those needs, who accept and forgive with open arms. Is this how you act toward your spouse?

At times you will have to point out aspects of your spouse's life that he or she still needs to work on. If your objective is only to shape that person to be what you want, your selfishness will detract from, rather than add to, the relationship. But, if you are honestly looking out for your mate's best interest, you are on the right track.

If you are not married, it may seem like you have a formidable task ahead of you. In two words: You do. Marriage cannot be approached lightly. God designed it to be a reflection of His character—a total, selfless, giving love with no strings attached. Just as the Father, the Son and the Holy Spirit are one, the husband and wife are to be unique individuals functioning as a single unit. "For this cause a man shall leave his father and his mother, and shall cleave to his wife; and they shall become one flesh" (Genesis 2:24).

As sinful people, we always will fall short of perfect unity in one way or another. But this is no excuse, no reason to quit trying.

Handle With Prayer

A love, marriage and sex relationship lived to the fullest is a joy and a celebration. It is a gift from God and a commitment to God and to each other.

Pray for the wisdom to be a godly husband and spiritual leader, one who makes his wife hunger for God. Pray for the wisdom to be a godly wife and supporter, one who makes her husband thirst for righteousness in his own life. Pray that God will make you the right person for someone else.

When you are seeking God, seeking to improve yourself and seeking the best interest of the other, your marriage will be fulfilling. It will bring out the best in each of you as never before.

FOOTNOTES

SECTION I
Chapter 1

1 *USA Today* (Oct. 12, 1984), p. 10A.
2 "Lot of Women Grinning and Bearing It," *USA Today* (Jan. 15, 1985), p. 1.
3 Leslie Linthicum, "The Hug or the Whole Thing?", *The Houston Post* (Jan. 16, 1985).
4 *USA Today* (Jan 15, 1985), p. 1.
5 Dorothy T. Samuel, *Love, Liberation and Marriage* (New York: Funk and Wagnalls, 1976), Preface.
6 Rollo May, *Love and Will* (New York: Dell Publishing Co., 1969), p. 40.
7 William H. Masters, Virginia E. Johnson, *The Pleasure Bond* (New York: Bantam Books, 1976), pp. 113-114.
8 *USA Today* (Oct. 12, 1984), p. 10A.
9 *USA Today* (Oct. 12, 1984), p. 10A.

Chapter 2

1 Evelyn Duvall and Rueben Hill, *When You Marry* (New York: Association Press, 1948), p. 1.
2 Duvall and Hill, *When You Marry*, p. 26.
3 Elof G. Nelson, *Your Life Together* (Richmond: John Knox Press, 1967) p. 18.
4 Bob Phillips, *A Humorous Look At Love & Marriage* (Eugene, OR: Harvest House Publishers, 1981), pp. 54-57.

Chapter 3

1 Matt Clark, "The Sex-Therapy Revolution," *Newsweek* (Nov. 17, 1980), p. 98.
2 "I am Loved" by Wm. J. and Gloria Gaither. © Copyright 1978 by Wm. J. Gaither. All rights reserved. Used by permission.
3 C. S. Lewis, *The Screwtape Letters* (Macmillan Publishing Co., New York, NY, 1961); p. 64.

Chapter 4

1 Claire Safran, "Troubles that Pull Couples Apart," *Redbook* (January, 1979), p. 83.
2 Terri Schultz, "Does Marriage Give Today's Women What They Really Want?" *Ladies Home Journal* (June, 1980), pp. 90, 150.
3 Carla Stephens, "50 Questions Before You Say, 'I Do' " *Christian Life* (September, 1979), p. 26.
4 Herbert A. Glieberman, "Why So Many Marriages Fail, " *U. S.*

News & World Report (July 20, 1981), p. 54.

5 *USA Today* (October 12, 1984), p. 11A.

6 Marilyn Elias, "Affairs: Women Look For Intimacy," *USA Today* (Nov. 6, 1984), p. 1D.

7 H. Norman Wright, *Communication: Key To Your Marriage* (Ventura, CA: Regal Books, 1979), p. 52.

8 Dwight Small, *After You've Said I Do* (Old Tappan, NJ: Fleming H. Revell, 1968), p. 51.

9 Cynthia Deutsch, "The Dangers of A Silent Partner," *Parents* (Oct., 1979), p. 24.

10 *Hamlet* Act i, sc. 3, 1. 68.

11 Richard B. Austin, Jr., *How To Make It With Another Person* (New York: MacMillan Publishing Co., 1976), p. 93.

12 David Augsburger, *Freedom of Forgiveness* (Chicago: Moody Press, 1973), p. 87.

13 David Augsburger, *Caring Enough To Hear and Be Heard* (Ventura, CA; Regal Books, 1982), p. 104.

14 H. Norman Wright, *More Communication Keys To Your Marriage* (Ventura, CA: Regal Books, 1983), p. 89.

15 Michelle Sandlass, "The Power of a Happy Positive Self-Image," *Glamour* (Jan., 1979), p. 120.

16 Dr. David Augsburger, *Caring Enough To Hear and Be Heard* (Ventura, CA: Regal Books, 1982), pp. 149-150.

17 Joyce Landorf, *Tough and Tender* (Old Tappan, NJ: Fleming H. Revell Co., 1975), p. 76.

Chapter 5

1 H. Norman Wright, *More Communication Keys For Your Marriage* (Ventura, CA: Regal Books, 1983), p. 90.

2 David Augsburger, *Caring Enough To Hear and Be Heard* (Ventura, CA: Regal Books, 1982), p. 74.

3 Richard Strauss, *Marriage Is For Love* (Wheaton, IL: Tyndale House Publishers, 1979), p. 87.

4 George E. and Nikki Koehler, *My Family: How Shall I Live With It?* (Chicago, IL: Rand McNally & Co., 1968), p. 27.

5 Jody Gaylin, "First-Year Fights," *Glamour* (Dec., 1979), p. 26.

6 J. Allen Petersen, *Before You Marry* (Wheaton, IL: Tyndale House Publishers, Inc., 1974), p. 43.

7 David R. Mace, *Getting Ready For Marriage* (New York: Abingdon Press, 1972), p. 71.

8 Wright, *More Communication*, pp. 127-128.

9 Leo Buscaglia in *USA Today* (October 12, 1984), p. 11A.

10 Margaret Lane, "Are You Really Listening?" *Reader's Digest* (Nov., 1980), p. 183.

11 Richard L. Strauss, *Marriage Is For Love*, p. 86.

12 H. Norman Wright, *The Pillars Of Marriage* (Ventura, CA: Regal
    Books, 1979), p. 86.
13 H. Norman Wright, *Communication: Key To Your Marriage* (Ven-
    tura, CA: Regal Books, 1974), p. 150.

Chapter 6

1 David Augsburger, *Caring Enough to Hear And Be Heard* (Ventura, CA: Regal Books, 1982), p. 20.

Chapter 7

1 Tim LaHaye, "How To Live Happily Ever After," *Christian Life*
   (Sept., 1979), p. 26.
2 Richard Strauss, *Marriage Is For Love* (Wheaton, IL: Tyndale
   House Publishing, 1979), p. 95-96.
3 Hal Linsay, *The Liberation of Planet Earth* (Grand Rapids: Zondervan Publishing House, 1974), pp. 170, 172.

Chapter 8

1 Richard Strauss, *Marriage Is For Love* (Wheaton, IL: Tyndale
   House Publishing, 1979), p. 17.
2 Gretchen Kurz, "Sexual Liberation; Is It Worth the Hassle?"
   Mademoiselle (August 1977), pp. 207-8.
3 Lonnie Barbach and Linda Levine, "How to Turn Good Sex Into
   Great Sex," *Mademoiselle* (October, 1980), p. 207.

Chapter 9

1 Sally Wendkos Olds, "Do You Have What It Takes To Make A
   Good Marriage?" *Ladies' Home Journal* (October, 1980), p. 202.
2 David R. Mace, "What Makes A Good Marriage?" *Family Guide
   To Good Living* (Woodbury: Bobley Publishing Corp., 1977), p.
   175.
3 H. G. Zerof, *Pitfalls Of Romantic Love* (n.p., n.d.), p. 166.
4 David Bogard, "Marriage Made In Heaven," *Decision* (June,
   1981), p. 8.

Chapter 10

1 Herbert J. Miles, *Sexual Understanding Before Marriage* (Grand
   Rapids: Zondervan Publishing House, 1971), p. 197.
2 Elof G. Nelson, *Your Life Together* (Richmond: John Knox Press,
   1976), p. 20.
3 David R. Mace, *Getting Ready For Marriage* (New York:
   Abingdon Press, 1972), p. 45.

Chapter 11

1 Sally Wendkos Olds, "Do You Have What It Takes To Make A Good Marriage?" *Ladies Home Journal* (Oct., 1980), pp. 76-78, 202-204.

2 Lorna and Philip Sarrel, eds., "The Redbook Report On Sexual Relationships: A Major New Survey Of More Than 26,000 Women and Men," *Redbook* (Oct., 1980), pp. 76-77.

3 Natalie Gittelson, "Happily Married Women: How They Got That Way, How They Stay That Way," *McCalls* (Feb., 1980), p. 36.

4 George A. Hughston and Michael J. Sporakowski, "Prescriptions For Happy Marriage: Adjustments and Satisfactions of Couples Married for 50 or More Years," *The Family Coordinator* (Oct., 1978), p. 323.

5 Robert B. Taylor, quoted in "Behind The Surge In Broken Marriages," *U.S. News & World Report* (Jan. 22, 1979), p. 52.

6 David Milofsky, "What Makes A Good Family," *Redbook* (Aug., 1981), pp. 60, 62.

7 Evelyn Millis Duvall, *Building Your Marriage—The Family Guide To Good Living* (Woodbury: Bobley Publishing Corp., 1977), p. 68.

8 James Robison, "Survey Hints Religion May Aid Sexual Enjoyment," *Chicago Tribune* (n.d., n.p.)

9 Herbert J. Miles, *Sexual Understanding Before Marriage,* pp. 76-78. [For Dr. Miles bases for his research, see his book *Sexual Happiness in Marriage*, Appendix I, p. 131; Appendix II, pp. 132-146.]

10 Josh McDowell, *His Image... My Image* (San Bernardino: Here's Life Publishers, Inc., 1984), pp. 126-129.

11 J. Allen Petersen, *Before You Marry* (Wheaton, IL: Tyndale House Publishing, 1974), p. 28.

Chapter 12

1 Don Osgood, *Christian Herald* (December 1976).

2 DPD Digest, IBM Corporation.

Chapter 13

1 Terri Schultz, "Does Marriage Give Today's Women What They Really Want?" *Ladies' Home Journal* (June, 1980), p. 91.

2 Urban G. Steinmetz and Bernard R. Weise, *Everything You Need To Know to Stay Married And Like It* (Grand Rapids: Zondervan Publishing House, 1972), p. 143.

3 Personal letter from Larry Burkett, Dec., 1984.

4 Ibid.

5 Dr. John MacArthur, Jr., from "Mastering Materialism" study notes.

SECTION II

Introduction

1 Evelyn Duvall and Reuben Hill, *Before You Marry,* (New York: Association Press, 1959) p. 36

Chapter 15

1 H. Norman Wright, *The Pillars Of Marriage* (Ventura, CA: Regal Books, 1979), pp. 41-42.
2 Evelyn Duvall, "Mature Enough To Marry," *The Marriage Affair* (Wheaton: Tyndale House Publishers, 1971), p. 17.
3 Ben A. Ard, Jr., and Constance C. Ard, *Handbook Of Marriage Counseling* (Palo Alto: Science and Behavior Books, Inc.), p. 289.
4 Jerry Adler, "The Science of Love," *Newsweek*, (Feb. 25, 1980), p. 89.
5 Kenneth Woodward, "What The Pope Is Really Saying About Sex And Marriage," *McCalls* (April, 1981), p. 192.
6 Howard Hendricks, "Yardsticks for Love" (lecture notes), p. 25.
7 George F. Gilder, *Sexual Suicide* (New York: Quadrangle, 1973), p. 72.

Chapter 16

1 Evelyn Duvall and Reuben Hill, *When You Marry* (New York: Association Press, 1948), p.35.
2 Dr. Richard Strauss, *Marriage Is For Love* (Wheaton, IL: Tyndale House Publishers, 1979), p. 35.
3 Elof G. Nelson, *Your Life Together* (Richmond: John Knox Press, 1967), pp. 68-69.
4 C.S. Lewis, *The Four Loves* (New York: Fontana, 1963), p. 104F.

Chapter 17

1 Larry Christenson, *The Christian Family* (Minneapolis: Bethany Fellowship, Inc., 1970), pp. 27-28.
2 Stanley L. Englebardt, "What Is This Thing Called Love?" *Reader's Digest* (June, 1980), p. 109.
3 John Powell, *Why Am I Afraid To Love?* (Niles: Argus Communications, 1972), pp. 25,27.
4 Albert Lee and Carol Allman Lee, *The Total Couple* (Dayton: Lorenz Press, 1977), pp. 75-76.
5 Madora Holt, "The Secrets Behind Successful Marriages," *Christian Science Monitor* (October 5, 1978), p. 17.

Chapter 18

1 Gary Inrig, *Quality Friendship* (Chicago: Moody Press, 1981), pp.156-157.
2 Inrig, *Friendship*, p. 156-157.
3 Kenneth S. Wuest, *The New Testament, An Expanded Translation* (Grand Rapids: Erdmans, 1981), p. 407.
Additional References:
The Christian Home, "Walking In Love," pp. 16-18.

Chapter 19

1 Walter Trobisch, *I Loved A Girl* (New York: Harper & Row,1963), p. 25.
2 Henry Brandt, *When A Teen Falls In Love* (Grand Rapids: Zondervan, n.d.), p. 27.

Chapter 20

1 Evelyn Duvall and Reuben Hill, *Before You Marry* (New York: Association Press, 1959), p. 33.
2 Charles R. Swindoll, *Commitment: The Key To Marriage* (Portland: Multnomah Press, 1981), p. 15.
3 Frank O. Cox, *Human Intimacy: Marriage, The Family and Its Meaning* (St. Paul: West Publishing Co., 1984), p.118.
4 Lawrence Crabb, Jr., *The Marriage Builder* (Grand Rapids: Zondervan Publishing House, 1982), pp. 33-34.
5 Herman Weiss and Judy Davis, *How To Get Married* (New York: Ballantine Books, 1983), p. 12.
6 Natalie Gittelson, "Happily Married Women: How They Got That Way, How They Stay That Way," *McCall's* (Feb., 1980), p. 36.
7 Frank O. Cox, *American Ways Of Love* (Los Angeles: West Publishing Co., 1978), p. 79.
8 H. Norman Wright, *Pillars Of Marriage* (Ventura, CA: Regal Books, 1979), p. 44.

Chapter 21

1 H. Norman Wright and Marvin Inmon, *A Guidebook To Dating, Waiting, And Choosing A Mate* (Irvine: Harvest House Publishers, 1978), p.17.
2 Harold J. Sala, "20 Commandments For A Better Marriage," *Christian Life* (Jan. 1979), p.53.

Chapter 22

1 Albert Lee and Carol Allman Lee, *The Total Couple* (Dayton: Lorenz Press, 1977), p. 54.

2 Kathleen Fury, "Sex and the American Teenager," *Ladies Home Journal* (March, 1980), p. 159.

3 Walter Trobisch, *I Loved A Girl* (New York: Harper & Row, 1963), p. 4.

4 Dr. Richard L. Strauss, *Marriage Is For Love* (Wheaton, IL: Tyndale House Publishers, 1979), p. 34-35.

Chapter 23

1 Robert B. Taylor, "Behind The Surge In Broken Marriages," *U.S. News & World Report* (Jan. 22, 1979), p. 53

2 Ibid.

3 Charles R. Swindoll, *Commitment: The Key To Marriage* (Portland: Multnomah Press, 1981), p.18.

4 Swindoll, *Commitment*, p. 18.

Chapter 24

1 David Gelman, "How Marriages Can Last," *Newsweek* (July 13, 1981), p. 73.

LET'S STAY -IN- TOUCH!

If you have grown personally as a result of this material, we should stay in touch. You will want to continue in your Christian growth, and to help your faith become even stronger, our team is constantly developing new materials.

We are now publishing a monthly newsletter called 5 Minutes with Josh which will

1) tell you about those new materials as they become available
2) answer your tough questions
3) give creative tips on being an effective parent
4) let you know our ministry needs
5) keep you up to date on my speaking schedule (so you can pray).

If you would like to receive this publication, simply fill out the coupon below and send it in. By special arrangement 5 Minutes with Josh will come to you regularly — no charge.

Let's keep in touch!

Josh

☐ **Yes!** I want to receive the free subscription to **5 Minutes with JOSH**

_____
NAME

_____
ADDRESS

_____
CITY, STATE/ZIP

SLC-2024

Mail To:
Josh McDowell
c/o 5 Minutes with Josh
Campus Crusade for Christ
Arrowhead Springs
San Bernardino, CA 92414